1937 Packard, Tom Stockhouse
1937 Packard One Twenty, Darvin and Becca Kuehl
1937 Packard Twelve, Neil Torrence
1937 Pontiac, Kenneth E. Havekort
1938 Chevrolet, Bob Stremmel
1938 Lincoln Zephyr, Clay Nichols
1938 Packard Eight, Armand Annereau
1939 Ford, Len Vinegard
1939 Lincoln Zephyr, Jerry Emery
1939 Packard, Ralph Geissler
1939 Plymouth, Walter Thomas
1940 Buick, Jim Bowersox
1940 Packard, Eugene Tareshawty
1941 Chevrolet, John Poochigian
1941 DeSoto, Donald E. Desing
1941 Ford, Henry and Joan Rehm
1941 Lincoln Continental, Harry Wynn
1941 Lincoln Zephyr, Clay Nichols
1941 Packard One Twenty, Ralph Geissler
1941 Plymouth, Joe Eder
1942 Buick, Domino's Pizza
1942 Lincoln, Harry Wynn
1947 Buick, Bill Schwonbeck
1948 Chrysler, Ray Bleeke
1948 Lincoln Continental, Van Brocken
1948 Nash, Ken Havekort
1949 Cadillac, Burnell Mille
1949 DeSoto, Bruce Kennedy
1949 Ford, Hugh Dixon
1949 Frazer, Arthur Sabin
1949 Hudson, Bob Hill
1950 Buick, Alan Moss
1950 Mercury, Jerry and Jackie Lew
1950 Oldsmobile, Bud Juneau
1950 Pontiac, Kenneth E. Havekort
1951 Frazer, Brooks Stevens
1951 Kaiser, Ed Hausgen
1951 Lincoln, Stephen McCarthy
1951 Mercury, Bob Ward
1951 Packard, Lew Trent
1952 Mercury, Bud Manning
1953 Buick, Kurt Fredericks
1953 Cadillac, James Garbe
1953 Cadillac Eldorado, Bob Hofmann
1953 DeSoto, Tim Graves
1953 Plymouth, Mearl Zeigler
1954 Cadillac Eldorado, Gary Robinson
1954 Hudson, Frederick J. Roth
1954 Oldsmobile, Bob Weber
1954 Packard, David Burkholder
1955 Cadillac Eldorado, Joe Malta
1955 Chevrolet, James R. Cahill

1955 DeSoto, Jeff Wells
1955 Oldsmobile, Norb Kopchinski
1955 Packard, Raymond and Marilyn Benoy
1955 Plymouth, Mervin Afflerbach
1955 Pontiac, Richard Bourgie
1956 Chevrolet, Gary Johns
1957 Chevrolet, Bill Bodnardchuk
1957 Chrysler 300, Richard Carpenter
1957 Dodge, Daryl Thomsen
1957 Mercury, Bob Rose
1957 Pontiac, Dick Hoyt
1958 Buick, Michael L. Berzenye
1958 Cadillac, Dr. Gerard DePersio
1958 Cadillac Eldorado, Art Gravatt
1958 DeSoto, Tim Fagan
1958 Edsel, Andrew Alphonso
1958 Oldsmobile, Mark Apel
1959 Buick, Palmer Carson
1959 Chrysler 300, Richard Carpenter
1959 Plymouth, George Dalinis
1959 Pontiac, Frank Ellis
1960 Buick, Rich Shick
1960 Cadillac Eldorado, Bill Hall
1960 Chevrolet, Terry Lucas
1960 Edsel, Mike Cowles
1961 Buick, Harold Lee Lockhart
1961 Chrysler, Ray Shinn
1961 Ford, Roger Randolph
1961 Mercury, Sam Scoles
1961 Oldsmobile, Roy Herbener
1961 Pontiac, Harold Liesenfeld
1963 Ford, Barry Norman
1964 Cadillac, Jim Bowersox
1964 Ford Thunderbird, Mike and Marge Tanzer
1964 Studebaker, Peter Bell
1965 Chrysler 300, Richard Carpenter
1966 Cadillac Eldorado, Jim Bowersox
1966 Chevrolet Corvair, Andrew Mesrausras
1967 Chevrolet Camaro, Ernest Gigliotti
1967 Ford Mustang, Ken Baker
1967 Plymouth Barracuda, Dave Bartholomew
1967 Pontiac GTO, Don and Linda Davis
1968 Mercury Parklane, Jim Ashworth
1969 Mercury Cougar, Jack Karleskind
1969 Plymouth Barracuda, Mary Lee Cipriano
1969 Pontiac Firebird, Mike Abbott
1970 Buick, Rick Shick
1970 Oldsmobile 4-4-2, Bob Weggenmann
1970 Plymouth Barracuda, Wayne Hartye
1970 Plymouth Barracuda, Joseph "Whitey" Eberle
1971 Dodge Challenger, Dale Lingle
1971 Oldsmobile 4-4-2, Dean Cardella

THE GREAT AMERICAN CONVERTIBLE

BY RICHARD M. LANGWORTH
AND THE AUTO EDITORS OF OF CONSUMER GUIDE®

BEEKMAN HOUSE

Louis Weber, C.E.O.
Publications International, Ltd.
7373 N. Cicero Avenue
Lincolnwood, IL 60646

Permission is never granted for commercial purposes.

Printed and bound in Yugoslavia by CGP Delo
h g f e d c b a

ISBN: 0-517-65581-0

This edition published by Beekman House, Distributed by Crown Publishers, Inc., 225 Park Avenue South, New York, New York 10003

Library of Congress Catalog Card Number: 88-60742

CREDITS

Principal Author

Richard M. Langworth

Photography

The editors gratefully acknowledge Chrysler Corporation: Chrysler-Plymouth and Dodge Divisions; Ford Motor Company: Ford and Lincoln-Mercury Divisions; General Motors Corporation: Buick, Cadillac, Chevrolet, Oldsmobile, and Pontiac Divisions; Henry Austin Clark; Roland Flessner; David Gooley; Sam Griffith; Bert Johnson; Bud Juneau; Milton Gene Kieft; Vince Manocchi; Douglas Mitchel; Nicky Wright.

Owners

Special thanks to the owners of the cars featured in this book for their enthusiastic cooperation. They are:
1927 LaSalle, Owen Hoyt
1928 LaSalle, William E. Stevens
1929 Duesenberg, Terry Radey
1929 Studebaker, Milford Curtis
1930 LaSalle, Larry Klein
1930 Nash, Dr. James Dunkel
1931 Chrysler, Bill Tinka
1932 Chevrolet, Tom Schay
1932 DeSoto, Alex and Beverly Dow
1932 LaSalle, Daniel Allen
1932 Marmon Sixteen, Knox Kershaw
1932 Packard, Mrs. Benjamin Caskey
1932 Studebaker, S. Ray Miller
1933 Auburn, Auburn-Cord-Duesenberg Museum
1933 Essex Terraplane, Wayne R. Graefen
1933 Stutz, Ernest J. Toth, Jr.
1934 Terraplane, Gene Davis
1935 Buick, Ed Goehring
1936 Auburn, Leo Oser
1936 Cord, William Plunkett
1936 Ford, Carol Neslodeh
1936 Hudson, Phil Kuhn
1936 Packard One Twenty, B. Kavoon
1937 DeSoto, Bruce Kennedy
1937 LaSalle, Ed Gunther

The Great American Convertible: What it is, Why it Survives

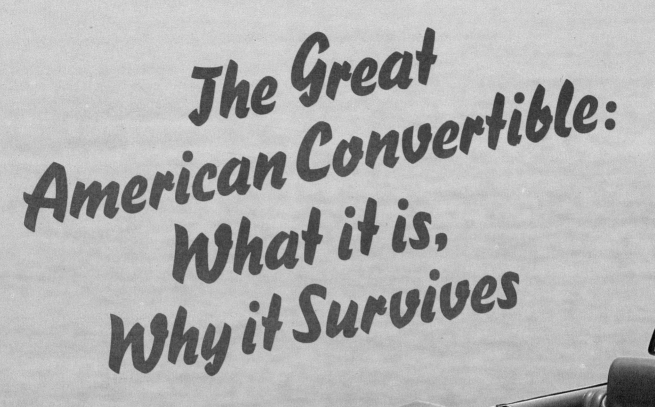

"Nothing, absolutely nothing," as Ratty would have told Moley had he had the requisite automotive experience, "beats messing about with convertibles." The American convertible is more than a car: It's a way of life, for no other body style combines the symbiotic pleasures of luxury and open-air motoring. Symbiotic? Yes, because a "ragtop" isn't all that luxurious in a freezing wind—something many owners, to their great dismay, encounter all too often.

But never mind: The convertible is unique. And as recent history shows, you just can't keep the old dear down.

Convertibles have blossomed again on the U.S. market and, barring a period as grim as the industry experienced in the late Seventies, it stands to remain a permanent part of the American scene.

Why? Obviously because the convertible is the *ne plus ultra* of cars as we know them—by a country mile the most desirable body style of all. A big part of that appeal is that it's usually the top of the line and thus (except for limousines) a given manufacturer's costliest and cushiest model.

But beyond these objective reasons lies the very simple and emotionally powerful fact that the convertible is simply more fun than other cars. You think of it as belonging to a golden, mellow autumn day, driven by a girl "whose face is brown with the sun," who "loves the cross of the wild and the tame," as Ned Jordan so eloquently put it in his romantic ad, "Somewhere West of Laramie." Convertible fans tend to forget that for about 300 days a year their cars cannot be enjoyed to the fullest unless they happen to live in southern California, Florida or Hawaii—or are slightly masochistic.

There's no mystery about the convertible's history, nor are its origins

Old or new, big or little, humble or mighty— Americans have always loved convertibles. *Above*: 1984 Dodge 600. *Pages 4-5*: 1969 Buick Skylark. *Pages 8-9*: 1958 Cadillac Eldorado Biarritz.

difficult to pinpoint. It all started in the late Twenties, when automotive body engineers contrived to make the roadster and touring car, then the dominant open body types, into something a bit more civilized by giving them folding tops and roll-up windows.

Nevertheless, we ought to be clear about how car people define a convertible as opposed to other open styles like roadsters, runabouts and phaetons. There's not much argument: A convertible must have a top that is permanently attached to a framework that you fold down—either by hand or with a power-assist—rather than remove completely (as you do the top of an MG sports car, for instance). Stricter pedants add that a convertible must have roll-up windows as well. The winsome Dodge Wayfarer was considered a "roadster" in 1949 (when it had side curtains), a convertible in 1950 (when its windows rolled up).

Of course, a convertible may have either two or four doors. As a two-door it was first referred to as a "cabriolet," later a "convertible coupe." Four-door styles have been called many things (including certain expletives on winter nights or in downpours when the electrics fail), but most have been termed "convertible sedans."

Manufacturers haven't helped latterday chroniclers, however. GM called its convertible sedans "convertible phaetons," which wasn't really accurate (a true phaeton seats five or more passengers and has a take-off top). Hudson for many years called its convertible coupes "broughams," which to the rest of the industry meant two-door sedan. Chrysler had a 1928 offering called "town cabriolet," by which it really meant town *car* (a limousine with open chauffeur's compartment).

Perhaps the simplest definition is that a convertible is a car that converts from fully open to fully closed via a mechanism permanently affixed to it. And the converting part need not always be soft, as Ford proved with its famous late-Fifties "retractables."

Extremists sometimes insist that a true convertible must also have pillarless construction (no fixed B- and C-pillars) and be fully open (no structural members above the beltline except for the windshield, of course). But this

would eliminate many prewar convertible sedans as well as postwar quirks like the 1949–51 Kaisers and Frazers and the 1950 Rambler. We won't go quite that far. And in the general context of engineering vocabulary, it would be wrong to do so. That its top folds back and windows roll down is enough to define a "true" convertible.

The definition must also include like-equipped two-seaters, though these have often been called "roadsters" even after their makers had given them convertible features. Of course, an open two-seater isn't automatically a roadster. By our definition, the 1955–57 Thunderbird and open Corvettes after 1955 are genuine convertibles, too.

Let us be equally clear about our purpose here, which is to provide a general survey of American convertibles by decade. For brevity and to avoid duplication, this book does not attempt detailed descriptions of individual models. Readers seeking such information are referred to two previous works by this author and the Auto Editors of CONSUMER GUIDE®: *Encyclopedia of American Cars 1930-1980* and *New Complete Book of Collectible Cars 1930-80*. Both cover convertibles as well their contemporary linemates. This book, however, does provide appendices listing annual convertible production by make and for the industry as a whole. The text provides pertinent facts on the design, engineering, performance and other traits of a model or series, primarily as they relate to the convertible versions, of course.

Just when did convertibles begin? Careful reviews of body offerings indicate that they arrived in model year 1927. And contrary to earlier accounts, they were built by far more than two or three companies. Research discloses convertibles (or "cabriolets") in the 1927 lines of no fewer than eight manufacturers: Buick, Cadillac, Chrysler, duPont, Lincoln, Stearns, Whippet and Willys.

So let us hie back 60 years and take up the breezy story of the American convertible at its birth.

Richard M. Langworth
Hopkinton, New Hampshire
October 1987

Who Invented the Thing, Anyway?

Eight makes introduced the "true" convertible body style for 1927, among them LaSalle, Cadillac's new companion car which debuted in March 1927.

LaSalle (*above*) continued its convertible in 1928,
but the hood now sported 28 fine vertical louvers.
Opposite: The 1928 Hudson convertible landau sedan
(*top*) sported a Murphy-built body. Pontiac's 1929
"New Big Six" convertible (*bottom*) sold for $825.

It may seem odd that eight different automakers—and a diverse lot at that—would all field America's first true convertibles in the same year. Analyzed individually, however, all had good reasons for pioneering the new style. GM had literally invented the automotive styling profession; Chrysler was famous for its skilled body engineers; Lincoln, through the influence of Edsel Ford, was fashion-conscious; and E. Paul duPont was ever willing to adopt the latest design ideas. (However, his Model E, which offered his first convertibles, totaled only 83 chassis for all bodies; it's mentioned with the others mainly for historical completeness.)

The remaining three—Stearns, Whippet and Willys—were part of the John North Willys empire, where the convertible idea had appealed early. Willys had bought Stearns, an established luxury-car producer, in December 1925; had brought out Whippet as a "junior Willys" the following year; and had long offered a wide variety of Willys models with conventional and sleeve-valve engines to an enthusiastic public. Throughout the Twenties, in fact, Willys-Overland never ranked below sixth in industry production and actually finished third in 1928, outpaced only by Chevrolet and Ford.

Thus it was that Willys-Overland listed numerous 2/4-passenger (rumble-seat) and four-passenger cabriolets under the Stearns-Knight, Whippet, Willys-Knight and Willys banners in 1927–29, usually in cheap and expensive trim alike. Spurred by the onset of the Depression, the respected and luxurious Stearns vanished in 1929, the Whippet in 1930. Curiously, Willys would never again field a convertible through its own demise as an automaker in 1955. Nevertheless, J.N. Willys deserves a good deal of credit for establishing the convertible early on in the low- and medium-price fields as well as in the upper market regions.

Other manufacturers of convertibles or cabriolets in 1927 built them in rather limited numbers but, unlike Willys, were destined to keep building them for a long time. Buick began with a single $1925 Master Six four-passenger convertible coupe, completing just 2373 examples for the model year. The volume for Cadillac's 2/4-passenger model (with an enclosed seat for two plus an open rumble for two

more) is unrecorded but must have been much lower, since at $3450 it cost a great deal more.

Chrysler's first convertible appeared in the new, *grand luxe* 1927 Imperial 80 series—a top-of-the-line two-seater whose roof folded via carriage-style landau irons. At $3495 it was outpriced that year only by the new Lincoln "Sport Convertible," a Brunn-bodied custom tagged at a cool $5000. A highlight of the bellwether New York Auto Salon in '27, this first Lincoln ragtop cost more than any other model in the line save an identically priced Dietrich phaeton.

Leaders quickly inspire imitators, and 1928 brought a raft of me-too convertibles. Auburn, Franklin, Graham, LaSalle, Nash, Peerless, Studebaker and Packard all had them; the pioneers, meantime, kept most of theirs going. Buick, however, now termed its con-

vertible a "Country Club Coupe," the first of many flowery euphemisms by which builders tried to identify just what it was that they'd stumbled upon. Conversely, the 1928 Chryslers included a "Town Cabriolet" that was actually a town *car*, not a cabriolet.

Such confusing terminology may have prompted the Society of Automotive Engineers, the governing professional association of the car industry, to formally adopt "convertible" as a standard body designation. In its statement, the SAE was satisfied to define this as "any open car with roll-up windows," while progress in manufacturing and design insured that convertible tops would be permanently attached to folding frameworks.

This convenience was a large part of the convertible's early appeal, not to mention sales. Since the mid-Teens, the roadster and touring car, once the

two most common open styles, had yielded in popularity to the closed "coach" and "sedan," which by the late Twenties were taking the bulk of sales industry-wide. Yet while fewer buyers still craved *al fresco* motoring, they were very much taken with the idea of tops that didn't need a small army to put up and down, and windows that got out of the way with only a couple of turns of a crank.

Packard, then America's premier luxury make, moved quickly into the new field plowed by rivals Lincoln and Cadillac, issuing factory convertibles on all three of its 1928 chassis: Eight and Custom Eight ($6000-$6300) as well as the soon-to-vanish Six ($3650). Customers took to them, and Packard would continue listing a wide array of

convertibles through 1942.

Auburn considered its "cabriolet" important enough to offer in five series, from price-leading 6-66 to the majestic eight-cylinder 115 on a 130-inch wheelbase. The latter, which could also be had as a roadster, phaeton or speedster, was a handsome car. Advanced, too, with Bijur pushbutton chassis lubrication and Auburn's first hydraulic brakes, yet it cost only $2195. With lesser versions priced as low as $1295, Auburn soon commanded a large slice of the convertible market, though the company had never built in great volume—and never would.

Nash, regularly among the top 10 producers in these years, built many more convertibles than Auburn, lead-

ing off in 1928 with a pair of "convertible cabriolets" in Special and Standard guise selling for $2500-$2600. These were pretty cars with classic upright styling, part of a Nash line that held over $3\frac{1}{2}$ percent of the market that year—the best Nash would ever do until 1949.

Pioneering Chrysler switched its production cabriolet body to the mid-range Model 72 chassis in 1928, but Imperial buyers now had the choice of two custom-bodied convertibles: a LeBaron 2/4-seater (39 built) and a Dietrich convertible sedan (10 built at $6795, the very top of the line). Similarly low in volume but new for their makers were the Franklin Airman 3/5-passenger convertible ($2925) and Graham-Paige's Senior Six ($2185)

The 1929 Duesenberg (*above*) was one of the most
elegant convertibles ever built. Also available
in 1929 were the attractive Oldsmobile Viking
(*below left*) and the luxurious Lincoln (*right*).

and Model 835 Eight ($2485) convertibles. Actual production isn't available for these or the Fisher-bodied LaSalle ($2550) and Peerless 6-91 ($1895), both 2/4-passenger rumble-seat cabriolets.

The more convenient new convertible style gained momentum in 1929 as Dodge, Hupmobile, Pontiac/Oakland and Studebaker joined the fray. So did two very small producers, Blackhawk and Gardner. Chrysler's 1928 purchase made a ragtop Dodge inevitable. It appeared at mid-1929 as a brace of cabriolets in the Senior Six line, along with other important innovations like automatic windshield wipers, stoplights, bumpers front and rear, interior courtesy lights, and the first downdraft carburetor fitted to an American car.

Hupmobile, then enjoying one of its last prosperous years, settled on three models and a slightly different approach. Where most medium-priced convertibles were 2/4-passenger jobs with rumble seats, Hupp offered its small Six with a choice of bodies: one with back seat, one without. The firm also offered full five-passenger capacity in its eight-cylinder Model M, after Buick's "Country Club"—only the second five-passenger two-door convertible. As we know now, it was this configuration that would soon dominate convertible ranks.

Like many others, Pontiac extended its final run of 1928 cars into 1929, replacing them with "genuine" '29s early in the calendar year. Called the "New Big Six," this second series ushered in Pontiac's first convertible, a rumble-seat cabriolet selling for $845. The catalog described its finish as "Shadow brown with orange trim striping and collapsible gray cloth teal top with tan mohair upholstery"—snappy. Other combinations were offered later. Some $400 upstream was an Oakland version with the same type body, though Pontiac's—with horizontal hood louvers and distinctive bisected radiator—looked nicer and sold better.

Studebaker was a serious convertible contender almost from the first. Winter 1927–28 brought announcement of Commander Regal and President State 2/4-passenger cabriolets with stylish bodywork and powerful engines, followed by a trio of four-seaters for a summer '28 revision (the new one was a Dictator Royal). South Bend also managed a little two-seat

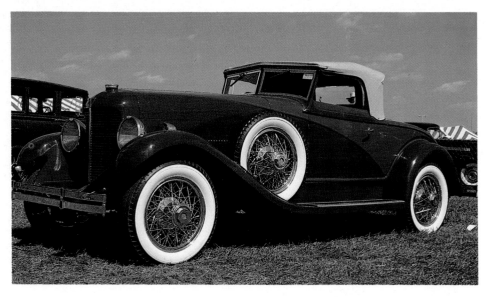

Two luxury convertibles for 1929 were the Dietrich-bodied Packard (*above*), with 145.5-inch wheelbase and $3350 price tag, and the very expensive and very rare DuPont Model G (*far left*), with body by Merrimac. List: $4360. More affordable was the 1929 Buick model 54CC DeLuxe convertible coupe (*left*), part of Series 129. It weighed a hefty 4085 pounds and listed at $1875; output reached 2021 units.

With the Dictator at the bottom, and the President
on top, the 1929 Commander Six was Studebaker's
mid-price offering. The "convertible cabriolet"
sold for $1495 and weighed 3215 pounds. A 248.3-
cid six with 74 horsepower provided motivation.

convertible coupe in its 108-inch-wheelbase Erskine line, one of the smallest of the new breed then available. Erskines never sold well, though, and the make would disappear in 1930.

Industry-leading Ford, at last returning to prosperity with the Model A, was the convertible's most important new adherent in 1929. At 16,421 units for the calendar year, its 2/4-passenger cabriolet beat the combined volume of all other new 1929 convertibles, making Dearborn the sales leader here, too. And so it would remain for most of the Thirties, building far more convertibles than anyone else—*including* Chevrolet, whose staid image somehow didn't suit the thing. In fact, despite some beautiful early-Thirties styling, Chevy wouldn't really be able to rival Ford's flathead ragtops for another 25 years.

Up to this point, roadsters, tourings and phaetons had continued to take the lion's share of open-car sales, mainly because most every maker still had them, whereas only a few had thus far offered convertibles. But the lion's share wasn't what it had been. Ten years before, open cars took 90 percent of the total U.S. market; by 1929 they were at 10 percent. After 1930 their typical share was three percent or less, where it would remain through mid-decade; by that time, most of Detroit had simply given up on the old styles.

The reason for that, of course, is that the convertible idea took hold. Though the process was gradual to be sure, it brought a merciless thinning in the ranks of other open styles. Signs of change were apparent as early as 1932, the last year when roadsters/tourings outsold convertibles. By 1939 they ac-

counted for only 0.3 percent of the market, whereas convertibles owned 10 times that much.

Still, the convertible had an uphill battle. It had barely come of age when America's greatest economic catastrophe set in, and though 17 nameplates listed convertibles for model year 1930, this relatively expensive and luxurious body style seemed out of place in a vastly diminished market. Economic necessity soon forced the more marginal manufacturers to drop convertibles as quickly as they'd embraced them. By decade's end, many of those companies were themselves gone for good.

The convertible survived, however, defying logic and the economic odds. The reasons it did—and some of its most splendid manifestations—are the subjects of our next chapter.

CHAPTER TWO:
1930~1939

Gold
Amidst the Gloom

The magic that was Auburn, Cord and Duesenberg—especially the sense of elegance (and the extravagance) that ever distinguished their patron, Errett Lobban Cord—brought convertibles from these marques quite early. Auburn, the humblest of the three, had been among the first practitioners of the convertible art, in 1928. A year later, soft-tops were among the first Cords, the rakish L-29s.

E.L. Cord was to the Twenties what Lee Iacocca is to the Eighties. Having made his mark as a super salesman at the Moon agency in Chicago, he became president of ailing Auburn in 1926 at the age of only 32. Against all odds, he soon had Auburn back in the pink. By 1930, with visions of rivaling GM and Ford, he'd added Duesenberg, engine-maker Lycoming, two coachbuilders and several other supplier companies to his budding empire.

But Auburn was always the lynchpin of that dream, and Auburn's Twenties prosperity simply couldn't continue in the Thirties' Depression austerity. Though its cars were good-looking, fast and bargain-priced, Auburn remained a relatively small automaker with too few dealers. Ultimately, E.L. Cord's mercurial management style created too many problems, and Auburn expired after 1936.

Nevertheless, like most of the other independents that didn't last this decade, Auburn built some of its finest cars in its final years. In fact, all Auburns from 1931 are certified Classics. Straight-eight power was Auburn's mainstay after 1930, with supercharged versions in 1935-36. But there was also the incredible 1932-34 Twelve—wretched excess for a troubled company but the cheapest V-12 in American history and, on its 133-inch wheelbase, an imposing car by any standard. Four-square styling characterized all Auburns through 1933, after which semi-streamlining took hold. Both remain pleasing to modern eyes.

The *crème de la crème* among open Auburns in this period, Gordon Buehrig's famous 1935-36 Speedster, is beyond our scope, but 2/4-passenger convertible cabriolets were listed in all series from 1931. Today they're hardly less scarce than Speedsters. Full model breakouts aren't available, but Auburn's total volume plunged from over 36,000 in 1931 to just 5500 registrations by '34. That means some pretty rare individual models, convertibles especially—true gold amidst the gloom of this failed marque. It was ever thus.

The Cord L-29 is equally rare and sought after, though it's doubtful there are any left to find. E.L. created it to fill the yawning price chasm between Auburn and the exotic Duesenberg; to assure good sales, he decreed an ultra-low stance for sensational looks. Indy race-car designer Harry Miller made that possible with his pioneering front-wheel drive system, adapted for production by Cornelius van Ranst. Alan Leamy came up with truly classic lines of majestic proportions. The L-29 was stunning in any form, but the 2/4-passenger cabriolet and five-seat phaeton sedan were naturally the most spectacular.

Alas, size means weight. With only a 115-horsepower Auburn straight eight to motivate it, the heavy—and tail-heavy—L-29 was none too good at climbing hills—or running fast on the flat. It wasn't cheap either, though prices were reduced after debut 1929 to perk up sales. By 1931 the cabriolet was down from $3295 to $2495, the phaeton to $2595. But sales didn't perk and production was halted in late '31 at about the 5000 mark (all bodies). The Cord wasn't finished, though, and we'll return to it later.

A-C-D appropriately shunned "factory" bodies for the Duesenberg Model J, offering custom styles exclusively from the mighty car's 1928 announcement. As most every enthusiast knows, they were truly magnificent. Rollston (later Rollson) and LaGrande began offering convertible styles in 1930. Murphy, that paragon of West Coast flair, had actually built one or two convertible coupes and sedans on 1929-registered J chassis, though the majority came along in 1930-32.

There was nothing like a Duesie regardless of body, but it was truly without peer in open form. Fred Duesenberg's brains and E.L. Cord's money produced what they—and many others—called with no exaggeration "the world's finest motor car." One reason: its locomotive-like 420-cubic-inch Lycoming straight eight, with twin-overhead camshafts driving four valves per cylinder to produce 265 horsepower—about twice the output of the industry's previous power leader, Chrysler. Equally imposing was the J's wheelbase: no less than 142.5 inches (sometimes stretched to 153.5 inches, though not for convertibles).

All Duesenberg Js were (and still are) the province of those above the "upper crust": stars rather than starlets, senators rather than congressmen, board chairmen rather than company presidents. More rarefied still were the customs you could count on fingers and toes: the long-wheelbase JN of Duesenberg's twilight years

(sometimes with open bodywork), the thrilling supercharged SJ and the legendary SSJ. The last saw only two examples, both LaGrande convertibles on abbreviated 125-inch chassis. The first was purchased off the showroom floor by film star Gary Cooper; the second was ordered by Clark Gable—probably because he couldn't bear the thought of being outclassed by friend "Coop." Both SSJs survive today—unquestionably among the most desirable and valuable American convertibles ever built.

No wonder. Only 470 Model J chassis were completed between 1928 and 1936. Though a high proportion originally carried convertible bodies, there are more soft-top models now because of blatant body switching.

Predictably, the company never made money with this formidable—and formidably expensive—masterpiece. But as Ken Purdy wrote, Fred Duesenberg had chosen "a good course and held unswervingly to it...With his mind and his two good hands, he had created something new and good and, in its way, immortal. And the creator is, when all is said and done, the most fortunate of men."

At the other end of the scale, the convertible began figuring into the dogfight between Ford and Chevrolet for the title of "USA 1." With introduction of the Model A in 1928, Ford had wrested the sales lead from Bill Knudsen's surging Chevy, only to lose it again in 1931. Not until the advent of the V-8 line in 1932 would Dearborn

head off Bill's car, and then only for a few years.

Offered in small numbers beginning in the A's second year, the jaunty 2/4-passenger convertible cabriolet was an established part of the Ford line by 1931. (Unlike most other body styles, however, it would be available only in standard trim through 1937, when it became a better-equipped DeLuxe.) Chevy, which had no counterpart before then, brought out a 2/4-passenger rumble-seat cabriolet in that year's new "Independence" series. At $595 and $615 respectively, both these cars were pricey, though not top of the line. Ford also built 4864 true convertible sedans, priced at $640 each; Chevy countered with 5634 two-door landau phaetons at $650 the copy.

Among the nine 1930 Essex Challenger models available was the Sun Sedan (*above*), which sold for $695. Its 58 horsepower paled in comparison to the 265 bhp of the elegant 1930 Duesenberg Model J Murphy Torpedo Berline (*below*).

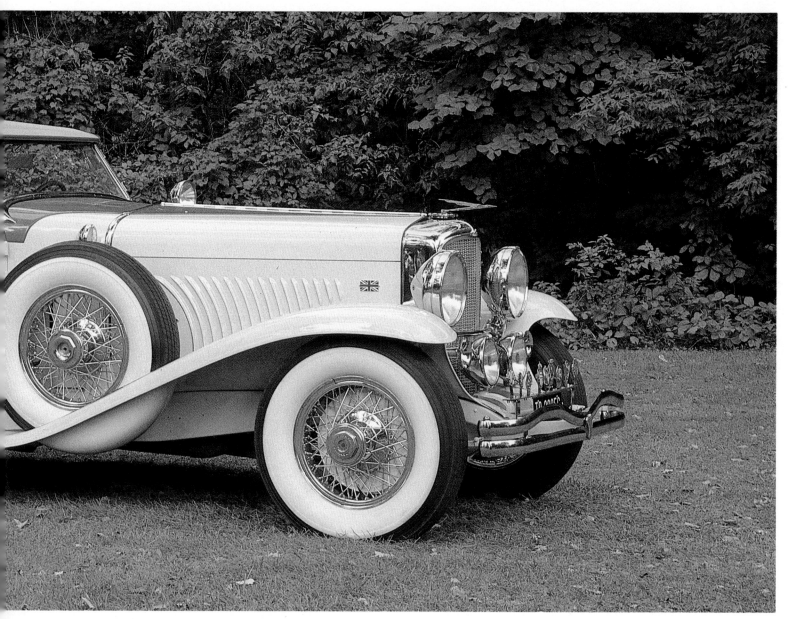

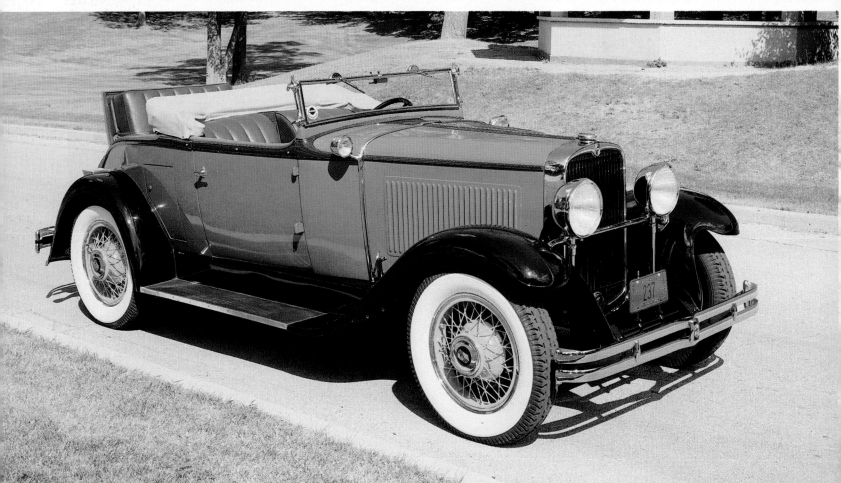

Through mid-decade, the two-doors' sales battle mirrored the general war, with Ford triumphant:

Cabriolet
Model Year Production

Model Year	Chevrolet	Ford
1931	23,077	13,706
1932	1,602	7,063[1]
1933	4,276	12,000[2]
1934	3,276	12,000[2]

[1] includes Standard and Deluxe models
[2] estimated from combined 1933-34 production

Chevrolet furloughed its cabriolet for 1935, then revived it in the restyled '36 fleet. The model continued selling poorly, however: never more than 4000 a year. Ford did much better, and even continued convertible sedans (which Chevy never bothered with) through 1939. Dearborn's speedy V-8 was clearly preferred by soft-top buyers—in retrospect, hardly surprising.

Even before the 1929 stock market crash, the Big Two had a rival in Chrysler Corporation. Founded by Walter P. Chrysler in 1924, it soon became a "full-line" producer with the 1928 acquisition of Dodge Brothers and the introduction of Plymouth and DeSoto that same year. Well known for handsome styling in its early days, the Highland Park company had been an early advocate of convertibles. Dodge and Chrysler had them in the Twenties. Plymouth and DeSoto got them in 1930.

A hotly competitive new Plymouth appeared for 1931, still with a four-cylinder engine but outclassing its rivals with "Floating Power"—engine mounts lined with heavy rubber to insulate them from the frame—a simple but remarkable innovation that gave Plymouth "the smoothness of an eight and the economy of a four." Chrysler's low-price make finished third in production for the first time that year and would remain there for the next quarter-century, aided by a switch from fours to sixes effective with the '33s.

Plymouth fielded Standard and DeLuxe series from 1932, and it initially issued convertibles in both. This was a shrewd departure from Ford/Chevy tactics, and it worked. While Chevy struggled to sell convertibles, Plymouth's slightly better-heeled customers took about 7000 a year in 1932-33. Then Plymouth restricted its rag-

Cadillac's companion make, LaSalle, sold the Model M convertible coupe (*blue car*) for $2590 in 1930. The '30 Nash rumble-seat cabriolet (*green car*) went for half that. The far costlier '30 Stutz Model M Convertible Victoria by Rollston (*above*) was powered by a 113-bhp Vertical Eight.

top to the DeLuxe line for 1934 and sales fell apart—curious, because the DeLuxe had previously outsold the Standard version. Successive restyles, attractive colors and handsome leather interiors didn't seem to help. In 1937, with the industry fast recovering from the Depression, Plymouth moved only 3110 convertibles.

As an experiment, Plymouth built 690 convertible sedans for 1932, but didn't field a production model until 1939. It was only a one-year stand and just 387 were built—Chrysler Corporation's last four-door convertible.

Its demise coincided with that of the great Walter Chrysler, who'd been ailing for several years. He died in 1940 of a cerebral hemorrhage at age 65. Many say the company's soul died with him, but some of the firm's finest hours lay ahead in the Fifties, Sixties and Eighties.

DeSoto and Dodge, Chrysler's midrange makes, offered small numbers of convertibles throughout the Thirties. The sole exception was the '34 DeSoto line, which relied exclusively on the advanced but controversial Airflow design that wasn't conceived with

a drop-top in mind. (It was just as well. The Airflow wouldn't have made a nice-looking convertible, and the body style just didn't fit the project goals of superior aerodynamics and all-steel "safety" construction, both of which were more readily accomplished with closed bodies.)

As is widely known, the Airflow never got off the ground. But contrary to long-accepted "wisdom," the reason was not so much styling (which many buyers liked) as production delays and unfounded rumors (some abetted by an envious GM), both of which damp-

ened initial interest and started thoughts that the Airflow was a "lemon." DeSoto thus managed only 14,000 model-year sales, prompting a hasty regrouping around more conventional Airstream styling for 1935.

Not that DeSoto had shown much flair for convertibles. Its open models were among the dullest around—if that's possible—though they cost close to $1000 and came in the more deluxe of two series. With its 1936 restyle, DeSoto attempted a convertible sedan that cost well over $1000 and thus sold only by the baker's dozen: 215 that

year, 426 the next, and just 88 in 1938, after which it was dropped. Perhaps as a result, DeSoto opted out of the soft-top business for 1939, then returned permanently with a convertible coupe in the handsome Ray Dietrich-styled 1940 line.

Dodge offered far more ragtops. In 1933, for example, it had no fewer than four, including a convertible sedan, all with a choice of six or eight cylinders. But the threadbare Thirties market demanded only about 1600 of them—hardly profitable. Accordingly, the division dropped its straight-eight

lines for '34, built diminishing numbers of convertible sedans (none after 1938) and, like DeSoto, forgot soft-tops entirely for 1939 (which probably accounts for that year's Plymouth convertible sedan).

Long overlooked among Classic-era convertibles are the singular Chryslers of 1931–33. If Chryslers were handsome before, stylist Herb Weissinger made them real head-turners with his unabashed copying of the Cord L-29. The similarity was most striking in the smoothly curved vertical-bar radiators of the top-line Im-

Chevy built 23,077 Independence cabriolets for 1931. They started at $615, but cost more when optioned up (*left*). By contrast, Chrysler produced only 700 CD convertibles that year at $1665 per copy (*above*).

25

perial and mid-range Eight/DeLuxe Eight, though the Cord's deft overall proportions and artful "clamshell" fenderlines were also in evidence.

Chrysler offered rumble-seat convertible coupes in each of its four series for 1931–33, and added convertible sedans with 1932's mid-year "second series" lineup. (A four-door convertible also appeared in the '31 Imperial CG series, though only 25 were built.) The 1933s were mildly altered in engine and wheelbase assignments and gained radiators tilted back a little, but their basic design remained largely intact.

A good thing too, for these were stylish cars, particularly in topless form, and smooth performers. The big straight-eight Imperials were the most impressive, of course, their long wheelbases (126-146 inches) making the most of what Weissinger had wrought. They were fully worthy of comparison with other Classics except in technical complexity—and price, which ranged from just $1325 for the 1933 Imperial Eight convertible coupe to a reasonable $3500 or so for LeBaron semi-custom styles. Other coachbuilders crafted one-off or few-at-a-time styles for various Chrysler chassis in these years, including Waterhouse in America and even a few European shops (the latter tending toward the more common Six and Eight platforms).

Having abandoned roadsters and phaetons after 1931, Chrysler joined DeSoto in 1934's Airflow debacle, though it didn't suffer as much because division managers had decided to retain the conventionally styled Six at the bottom of the line (a hedge, perhaps, but prudent, as events proved). This offered Chrysler's only folding-roof models that year: Six convertible coupe ($815) and Custom Six convertible sedan ($970). Like DeSoto, Chrysler bolstered Airflows for '35 with less radical Airstream models, but with eight as well as six cylinders (DeSoto was strictly sixes in this period). Convertible coupes and sedans arrived only as Eights, but the Airflow's steady decline prompted the addition of six-cylinder versions for '36.

Clockwise from left: The stylish 1931 Graham Model 822 Custom Convertible, $1635; 1932 Cadillac five-passenger All-Weather Phaeton, $3495; 1931 Ford Model A Convertible Sedan $640; 1931 Plymouth PA convertible coupe, $625.

The Airflow bowed out after 1937, the year other Chryslers were restyled with ungainly barrel-like fronts. The '38 fleet brought the return of non-Airflow Imperials and Eights, but other models were only a bit less awkward than they'd been the previous year. Much smoother lines marked the all-new '39s—but there were no convertibles, Chrysler emphasizing coupes and sedans with fancy trim and, for the Hayes-bodied victoria, distinctive rooflines. But the absence was only temporary, and convertible coupes would return for 1940.

For those intrigued by statistics, the Thirties was a time of stability for the convertible coupe and sedan. They had long since become "specialty models,"

shrinking from a dominant 83-percent market share in 1920 to just 10 percent by '29. In the Depression years they accounted for about three percent of total sales, about one percent after 1936 according to the National Automobile Chamber of Commerce (though the latter apparently included roadsters and touring cars, making the actual market penetration for true convertibles even less). Convertibles then recovered to 2-3 percent through decade's end; about 95 percent were two-doors.

With all this, you might wonder how convertibles survived past the Thirties. Since more were offered during the depths of the Depression than in recovery 1936–37 and 1939–40, they were clearly on the wane by mid-decade, the four-door in particular. (Some low-volume independents even lost money on them.) The reason isn't hard to divine: growing buyer preference for the greater safety and comfort of closed bodies, which advanced rapidly in the Thirties via features like all-steel construction, integral trunks, and door ventwings for "no-draft" ventilation. Still, the convertible did not die.

Why? The answer seems to be the perennial one long advanced by its proponents: The convertible was needed—not for profits but sheer sales appeal, the luster it lent to the workaday models standing next to it on showroom floors. The convertible was a symbol: always the best, the most luxurious, the most costly model in each maker's line, from Chevrolet to Cadillac, Lincoln to Ford. And remembering that most people were struggling with the mere basics of life at the time, the convertible served the important psychological purpose of assuring them that happy days would indeed be here again. In other words, the convertible ultimately became something to live for, a romantic reward for the hard times now endured. Hope meant much in the Thirties—about the only currency many folks had.

General Motors, grounded for a decade on Alfred Sloan's marketing dictum of "a car for every purse and pocketbook" and thus the master at parting money from consumers, continued to offer more convertibles than most anyone else—and more variety within each of its makes. The glamorous convertible sedan (which GM usually called "convertible pha-

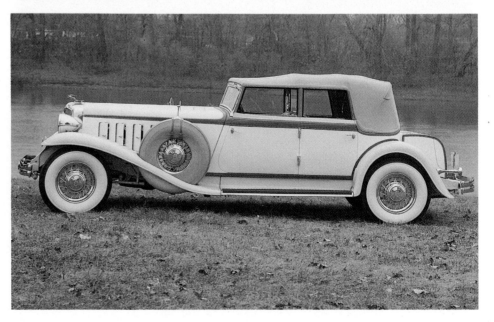

eton") was another of the firm's stocks-in-trade (except at Chevrolet). Of course, GM had more employee mouths to feed and thus perhaps needed the allure of convertibles more than, say, Studebaker, whose sales tended to rely more on buyer loyalty than outright value for money or even innovative styling and engineering.

As noted (Chapter 1), Cadillac and LaSalle, GM's top-line makes, had been among the first with true con-vertibles in the late Twenties. Cadil-lac's fabulous Sixteens and Twelves were offered with a vast array of fac-tory and custom bodies, including con-vertibles as a matter of course. There was always a convertible coupe in Cadillac's "basic" eight-cylinder line, usually priced competitively. The 1933 edition, for example, cost $2845, just $50 above the relatively spartan road-ster—though both represented a good year's pay for the average worker.

But it's the big multi-cylinder Cadil-lacs that everyone remembers, per-haps because these models were rela-tively uncommon after 1930–31, when they sold about 9000 units combined. Staggeringly expensive, they seemed almost vulgar in an era of widespread misery. (Other big luxury cars were shunned for the same reason. Even many of those who bought them often drove around in something less pre-tentious.) Later, their engines were

Chevy called its '32s Confederates, here a $500
DeLuxe sport roadster (*below*), 8552 produced.
Opposite, from top: '32 Auburn Eight, 100 bhp for
$795; '32 DeSoto New Six Custom roadster, $775,
894 built; '32 Chrysler convertible sedan.

outmoded by advancing technology. For example, the introduction of precision-insert conrod bearings helped eliminate the knock and high-speed engine wear that originally enticed wealthy types away from eights. Cadillac's Twelve thus vanished after 1937; the Sixteen somehow managed to hang on through 1940, though it seemed a relic of another age by then.

Nineteen thirty-four brought a deftly restyled Cadillac and a new LaSalle. The latter, born in 1927 as a junior Caddy with a smaller V-8, now became a sort of glorified Buick: cut $1000 in price, given an Oldsmobile L-head straight eight and, to its credit, GM's new "Knee-Action" independent front suspension. At least it looked somewhat like the smoother, more modern new Caddy. The LaSalle two-passenger convertible coupe, a glorious expression of money-talks class consciousness in 1933, had sold for about $3000 over the previous few years. The 2/4-passenger convertible of 1934 sold for $1695, same as the

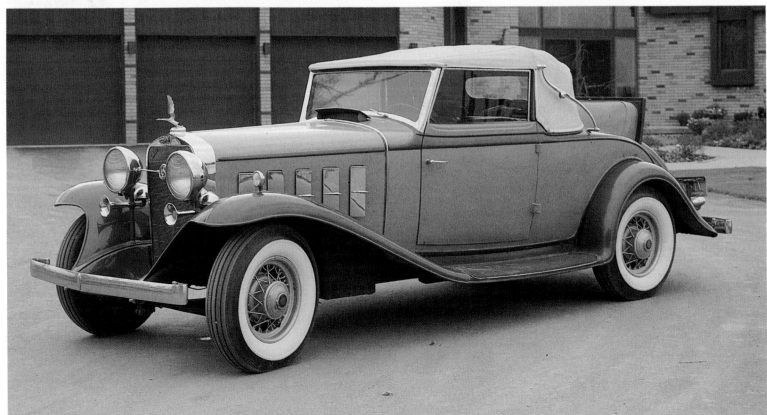

Opposite page: Marmon ended automotive production with the magnificent Sixteen, of which only 390 were built, here a 1932 convertible sedan (*top*). The '32 LaSalle convertible coupe sold for $2545 (*bottom*). *Below, clockwise from top*: '32 Essex Pacemaker, $845, built by Hudson; '32 Lincoln, body by Dietrich; '32 Plymouth PB, $690; '32 Nash, Model 981, $1325; '32 Ford V-8 Model 18, $610.

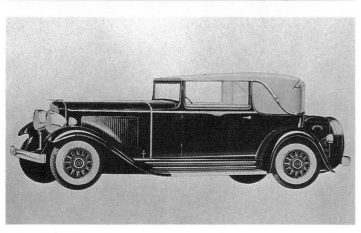

four-door sedan (suggesting GM purposely took a loss on it). Better still, it weighed 700 pounds less, to the benefit of performance.

LaSalle retained convertible coupes for the rest of the decade. Convertible sedans were also available from 1937, when Cadillac power returned. Prices were cut further in later years to encourage sales. The soft-top was down to $1255 by 1936, a long way from the heady sums of 1927–33. But Cadillac's medium-price Depression-fighter was a terminal case, being slowly squeezed out of its market by Buick as the economy inched toward recovery. Thus, only 855 two-door and 265 four-door convertibles were built for 1938; the respective 1939 figures were 1056 and 185. LaSalle's last hurrah came with the 1940 models, again adroitly styled by GM's Harley Earl. In some ways, they were the best LaSalles since the first ones.

Buick, Olds and Pontiac fared better than LaSalle, both generally and with convertibles. Buick was GM's convertible king, largely because it covered the widest market in the company. By 1931 the division was established with a four-series lineup (50, 60, 80 and 90) spanning $1000-$2000—which was quite a span in those days. Two years later it had a convertible in each line save the Series 90, which got one for '34. With the '36s came the now-familiar Special, Century, Roadmaster and Limited names. By that point, Buick usually proffered five or six convertibles a year, including four-door "phaetons" in the two senior series, plus Special and Century versions in 1937–38.

For most of the decade, Buick's annual soft-top production was 1500-3500 units, the majority being Special and Century convertible coupes. Phaetons were discarded after 1938 and saw far fewer copies: that year just 946 Specials, 219 Centurys and 411 Roadmasters.

Oldsmobile and Pontiac, with narrower market assignments and considerably trimmed lineups after 1933, built fewer soft-tops in this period. Nevertheless, Olds fielded at least one convertible in each series each year save 1934, when an eight-cylinder model was its lone entry. Pontiac offered but a single six-cylinder series in 1931, added a V-8 line for '32 (an extension of recently deceased Oakland), then went to straight eights for 1933–34. Each of these contained a convertible. Pontiac then blossomed into two Sixes and an Eight for 1935–36, each with a version of what it called a 2/4-passenger cabriolet.

In strict Sloan fashion, Pontiac convertibles usually sold for $800-$900, Oldsmobiles for about $900-$1100, this at a time when $100-$200 was a big difference. We should also not forget that Oakland, Pontiac's parent, had a convertible in its swan-song '31 line, priced at $995.

Unlike Buick, Pontiac and Olds bothered with convertible sedans only from time to time: Pontiac in 1937–38, Olds in the big 98 series of 1940–41. The latter was impressive on its 125-inch wheelbase and cost the world for an Oldsmobile: about $1600. This may explain why production ran to only 50

Opposite page: The Depression took a heavy toll on all auto makers, but Packard was still building genuine luxury cars, like this 1932 model (*top*). Studebaker (*bottom*) and Auburn (*below*) were also having a tough go of it in '32, but still turned out some memorable medium-priced convertibles.

units in the first year and 119 in the second.

The big guns among Thirties independents were Hudson (helped immeasurably by its offshoot Essex and Terraplane makes), Studebaker (when not in receivership) and Packard (after 1935, when it became a volume manufacturer by dint of the successful, lower-priced One Twenty). Hudson had popularized the closed coach as an Essex model in the Twenties, but stuck with the traditional roadster and touring until 1932, when it finally switched to convertibles for both the Hudson and Essex lines.

The big Hudson changed as dramatically as LaSalle once the Depression set in. Volume plummeted from a rollicking 300,000 units in 1929 to barely 40,000 four years later. Handsome and exciting though they were, the topline Hudsons just wouldn't sell. Adding insult to injury, Biddle & Smart, the make's long-time coachbuilder, was forced to close in 1930. Hudson's classic four-square styling ended three years later, accompanied by the return of six-cylinder power. Transitional 1934–35 models were followed by very modern, all-new '36s with skirted fenders, tall and rounded die-cast grilles and all-steel bodies.

Hudson limited itself to a single convertible in 1932–33, then listed one or more in most series. By 1938, convertible coupes and broughams were offered in a reabsorbed Terraplane line (DeLuxe and Super models) as well as in the senior 112, Custom Six and Deluxe Eight series. All were two-doors. Convertible coupes had a single bench seat for three; broughams were conventional six-seaters.

The low-price Essex had helped Hudson rise as high as third in the industry in 1927, but couldn't sustain itself after the Great Crash. What kept Hudson going was the smart and speedy Terraplane, an Essex offering in 1932–33, a separate make in 1934–37, a Hudson series in 1938 (after which the name was discarded). Terraplanes would generally do up to 80 mph and 25 miles per gallon yet cost as little as $425; convertibles were priced almost $200 higher, though. Adding to its appeal was an extra-cost eight-cylinder evolution of the original Essex Six, offered beginning in 1933.

The first Essex convertibles, Pacemaker and Terraplane, arrived for 1932. All Essex models were called Terraplane the following year, when a convertible was cataloged in each of the line's five series. Models were then cut and the Eight dropped as Essex disappeared and Terraplane became a separate make, but there were usually

The '33 Essex Terraplane Deluxe Eight convertible coupe (*below*) was fast, cost only $765. *Opposite, clockwise from top*: '33 Stutz DV-32 convertible coupe , '33 Cadillac V-16 Fleetwood Victoria, '33 Nash cabriolet, '33 Ford DeLuxe cabriolet, '33 Buick Series 80 convertible phaeton.

36

two convertible coupes each year and, in 1937, convertible broughams too. Of course, the open cars sold for much more than the average Terraplane: $725-$845 in 1937, for example, when closed cars started at $595. But their numbers and variety reflected well on the Terraplane's sporty and youthful personality.

Studebaker entered the Thirties with a broad lineup, though the economic malaise soon put paid to a good many models. It also nearly wiped out Studebaker. By 1933, the successive failures of side ventures Erskine and Rockne plus the purchase of Pierce-Arrow had put the old firm in receivership. Production executive Harold Vance and sales v.p. Paul Hoffman labored to pull it out, dumping Pierce and rebuilding the company's credit while working on more salable cars.

The Studebaker line was down to only three series by 1934: Dictator Six and Commander and President Eight. But this is misleading, for each comprised several sub-series: standard, Regal, St. Regis, Custom, plus the restyled "Year Ahead" '35 models that arrived in July 1934. Vance and Hoffman were concentrating on volume sellers, so there were "just" six convertibles: standard and Regal versions in each main line. But with only minimal demand, all were dropped for 1936, reflecting the continuing need for greater standardization and reduced production costs.

Meantime, Studebaker was planning the Champion, the low-price car that would return it to financial health in 1939. Still, this and other models would appear only as coupes and sedans, and with one brief exception, Studebaker would build nothing but closed cars through 1946.

But that exception was a dandy: a convertible sedan in the 1938–39 Commander and President series. Big and impressive, it sold for a whopping $300-$350 more than the next costliest model in each line. The predictable results were meager sales and very low production, making these some of the rarest and most desirable prewar Studeys for today's collectors.

Studebaker's future partner Packard probably experienced the greatest image change of any independent in the Thirties. From a maker of luxury cars "for a discriminating clientele," Packard moved gingerly downmarket with the Light Eight of 1932, then aggressively with the One Twenty of 1935 and the Six of 1937. These do-or-die medium-price models not only saved the company's hide but made Packard a significant contender in the annual production race for the first time. From its accustomed 18th place and an almost negligible 4803 units in 1933, Packard leaped to a strong eighth and a record 123,000 cars by 1937. The One Twenty ("Eight" in 1938), accompanied by the Packard Six after 1936, accounted for well over 90 percent of production. Both were offered as convertible coupes. The One Twenty was also available as a convertible sedan—and thereby hangs an interesting tale.

One Twenty convertible sedans carried a body plate reading "Dietrich," and some concluded that the great coachbuilder, who'd created so many magnificent senior-Packard bodies in past years, was responsible. This was precisely Packard's intent, but there was no connection. Ray Dietrich had left Dietrich, Inc. in 1930; by the time the One Twenty appeared, he was working on 1937–38 models for Walter Chrysler. But Murray had absorbed Dietrich, Inc. and continued to use the name. "Some of my leftover designs

Opposite, clockwise from top: Convertibles for 1934: Dodge DeLuxe Six, Buick Series 60, Cadillac sedan, Cadillac coupe, Auburn Eight. *This page*: The '34 Ford DeLuxe "roadster" (*top*) sold for $525, while a '34 Lincoln V-12 convertible coupe (*above*) ranged from $3400 to $5600 or more.

were actually completed by Murray and that's how the name went on the cars," Dietrich said later. "But I don't remember any lines of mine on a One Twenty. Murray, however, had established the practice by now, and they went ahead with it. How could I fight the Packard Motor Car Company? I had to trust their honesty, figuring there was honesty among thieves. But if they stole my name, I was very happy. The publicity didn't hurt!"

Packard naturally offered convertible coupes on its senior Eight and

Twelve chassis throughout the decade, though they were a very small percentage of a total volume that itself was small. Record 1937, for example, produced 115,500 Sixes and One Twentys against 5793 Super Eights and 1300 Twelves. The grand old Twelve, once queen of the line and a standard for America, vanished after model year 1939 and only 446 assemblies.

Among the smaller independents, Willys built no convertibles after 1930, while Hupp and Graham (formerly

Graham-Paige) produced a handful and Nash rather more. Hupp had its best year ever in 1928, registering over 50,000 cars, but wouldn't reach five figures after 1932 despite Raymond Loewy's handsome and advanced 1934 "Aerodynamic" design. The firm took a hiatus in mid-1936, reopened fitfully in 1937-38, then closed for good.

Hupp released its first convertibles in 1929 and generally had one in each series each year, variously calling it convertible coupe, convertible cabriolet and roadster cabriolet. Hupp's last

The Terraplane was considered quite a good looker in 1934, especially with the top down (*left*); it was available as a Special Six or Major Six with 80 or 85 horsepower. The '34 Buick Series 60 convertible phaeton (*below*) boasted 100 bhp and listed at $1675, but only 575 were built.

convertibles appeared in conventionally styled six- and eight-cylinder series for 1934.

Graham, whose history parallels Hupp's, dropped all its soft-top models after 1937. This automaker also had its best year before the Depression, then entered the Thirties with too many models for the shrunken market: sixes and eights in five series. Sales were down to 20,000 by 1931, then dropped by half over the next two years.

Graham produced its best convertibles in its leanest years. Notable was the Blue Streak Eight of 1932, beautifully sculpted by Amos Northup, creator of the '31 Reo Royale. The Blue Streak's skirted fenders prefigured an industry trend, and its 245-cid straight eight boasted an advanced aluminum cylinder head. The convertible, a 2/4-seater, came only in DeLuxe trim for 1932; a Standard model was added for 1933–34 along with six-cylinder running mates.

For 1935, Graham unleashed the Super-charged Custom Eight, America's first popular-price "hyperaspirated" car, packing 135 horsepower. Over the next six years, Graham would build more blown production cars than anyone else before, but it wasn't enough to insure the future. The 1936 line comprised sixes only, normal and supercharged, including standard and Custom Supercharger convertibles. These continued through 1937, after which Graham abandoned soft-tops and pinned its

Opposite page: The '35 Buick Series 60 convertible coupe (*top*) cost $1495; 111 were built. The Auburn (*bottom*) came with six or eight cylinders and, if desired, a supercharger. *This page, from top*: Ford priced the '35 DeLuxe convertible sedan at $580; output reached 6073. Only 41 Brunn-bodied Lincoln five-passenger convertibles were built for 1935. LaSalle offered two convertibles in 1935 at $1325 and $1545. Cadillac V-8 convertible prices started at $2445.

hopes—in vain, as it turned out—on the odd "Spirit of Motion" design now widely known as the "Sharknose."

Mention of the last Hupps and Grahams inevitably leads us to the second and final Cord, the great 810/812 of 1936–37. Bodies for the abortive rear-drive Hupp Skylark/Graham Hollywood of 1940–41 were made using dies obtained after Cord Corporation's collapse, but all were sedans; the 810/812 convertibles weren't similarly reincarnated (except for a prototype Skylark).

Like its L-29 predecessor, the 810 employed front-wheel drive but was far more compact and maneuverable, thanks to a Lycoming V-8 with 115 bhp. The 1937-model 812 was little changed apart from optional availability of a Schwitzer-Cummins supercharger that boosted power to 170—an astounding 190 with the "high-boost" package. So equipped, an 812 would do nearly 110 mph and 0-60 mph in 13 seconds, which made it among the fastest of prewar American cars.

But the second-generation Cords are mainly remembered for their predictive, Gordon Buehrig styling—smooth "coffin-nose" hood, wrapped "venetian blind" radiator louvers, graceful body lines. There were innovations aplenty: the industry's first concealed headlamps and fuel filler, dual taillights, a separate license-plate lamp, full wheel covers. All were advanced for the day and particularly heartening after the grim early Thirties.

There were two 810/812 convertibles, both two-doors: the aptly named Sportsman, a two-seat cabriolet, and a four-passenger four-window "convertible sedan" called Phaeton. They were relative bargains, too, at about $2600. Alas, production delays and mechanical woes doomed Cord's comeback, and relatively few 810/812s were sold.

Nash was one of the handful of independents that would survive these difficult years. It did so by merging with the Kelvinator appliance firm in 1937, which brought a bonus in the person of Kelvinator's cigar-chomping president, George Mason. Though founder Charles W. Nash remained nominally in charge, Mason increasingly made the decisions. They were usually the right ones.

Early-Thirties Nashes were sump-

Opposite, clockwise from top left: Plymouth and Pontiac for '35. Some '36s: Chevrolet Standard, 3629 built; Auburn two-door, $995-plus; Auburn 852 Supercharged four-door, $1725. *This page, from top*: Cadillac Fleetwood, $2745; Ford convertible sedan, $780, 5601 built; Nash 400 DeLuxe, $800.

43

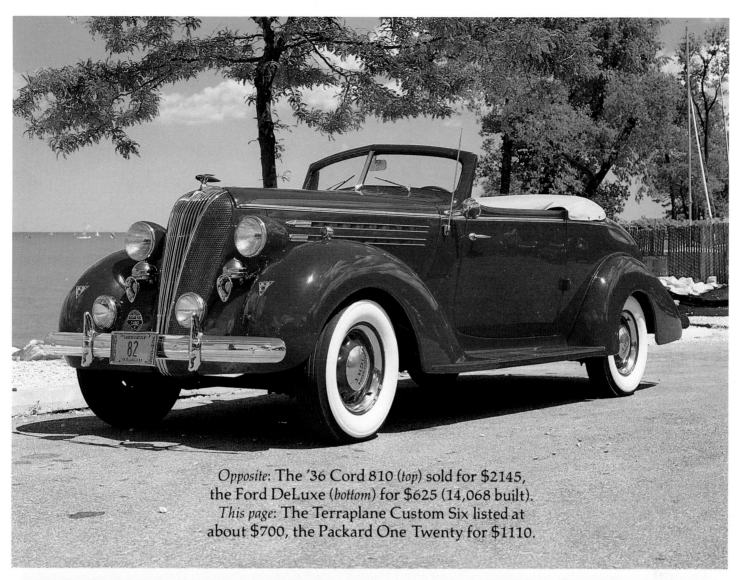

Opposite: The '36 Cord 810 (*top*) sold for $2145,
the Ford DeLuxe (*bottom*) for $625 (14,068 built).
This page: The Terraplane Custom Six listed at
about $700, the Packard One Twenty for $1110.

Above, clockwise from top left: The '36 Pontiac
DeLuxe Silver Streak cost $810; the Oldsmobile
Six, $805 (2136 built); the '37 Hudson Custom
Eight, $1260; and the Cadillac Series 70
Fleetwood, $3005. The '37 DeSoto Six convertible
sedan (*right*) boasted 93 horsepower. It listed at
$1300, but only 426 found buyers.

tuous, beautifully styled cars with many special features. Notable was "Twin Ignition," meaning two sets of sparkplugs/points/condensers/coils operating from a single distributor; overhead valves, an idea Charlie Nash probably got when he managed Buick; and nine main bearings for all straight eights. Styling was classically upright through 1933. A more streamlined group of '34s previewed 1935's still-swoopier "Aeroform" design with rounded lines and pontoon fenders. Successive facelifts belied its promise, however, and Nashes weren't really pretty again until 1939, appearing with flush-fit headlights and a slim vertical prow.

Through 1934, Nash soft-tops were conventional rumble-seat cabriolets and convertible sedans. Convertibles vanished with the '35 restyle (and a drastic, Depression-inspired model cutback), but an appropriately smooth 3/5-passenger cabriolet joined the '37 line, offered as a low-price Lafayette 400 and as a plush Ambassador Six and Eight. For many enthusiasts, the fine-looking '39 Ambassador Eight, on the longest (125-inch) wheelbase, is the most desirable late-prewar Nash, though it's no substitute for the superlative 1930–32 Twin Ignition Eights and Ambassadors with their impeccable lines and proud radiators.

Announced in the improving economic climate of 1939 was a new Ford make that's with us still: Mercury, named for the speedy "messenger of the gods." The brainchild of company president Edsel Ford, it was Dearborn's first direct competitor to GM's B-O-P trio and the Dodge/DeSoto duo from Chrysler. Compared to that year's Ford, the first Merc was just a little larger, more powerful, and accordingly more expensive, and ad writers waxed poetic over its column-mounted gearlever. But it was a good seller. The market called for about 75,000 of the '39s, divided among three sedans and a five-seat "convertible club coupe," a $1018 top-liner. Mercury volume would continue at this level through 1941.

Like main rivals Packard and Cadillac, Ford's luxury leader, Lincoln, cataloged a plethora of factory and custom bodies for its big L, K, KA and KB chassis of 1930–35. This naturally included convertible coupes and sedans, mainly supplied by the likes of Brunn, Dietrich and LeBaron. All were predictably scarce: in 1934, for example,

just 25 Brunns, 45 LeBarons and 25 Dietrichs. As with Cadillac's Sixteen, the lush Lincoln K and its big V-12 would be built through 1940 in rapidly diminishing numbers, which made for individual open models as rare as any in this period.

Again like its rivals, Lincoln weathered hard times by fleeing to the medium-price field, but with a far more radical car: the 1936 Zephyr. Based on a rear-engine concept by John Tjaarda, it emerged with a conventional chassis and the most balanced streamlining yet seen from Detroit—far prettier than the Airflow's, for instance—a tribute to Edsel Ford and E.T. "Bob" Gregorie. It was also the first car in which aircraft-type stress analysis actually proved the advantage of unit construction. At 3300

pounds, the Zephyr was both lighter and stiffer than most comparable cars. Its powerplant, a 100-bhp L-head V-12 derived from Ford's flathead V-8, proved troublesome, but sales took off as Lincoln, like Packard, became a high-volume make for the first time in its history.

Zephyr body styles initially comprised the expected coupe and sedan. Convertibles didn't appear until 1938, but they were worth the wait: two- and four-door models that benefitted from that year's effective facelift and longer wheelbase. The basically similar '39s were further improved via hydraulic brakes (belatedly adopted across the board in Dearborn) and a cooler-running V-12. Though worthy collectibles in their own right, these open Zephyrs led to an even more

coveted convertible: the first-generation Continental, not in production until 1940, though the prototype built for Edsel Ford was based on a '39 Zephyr.

Less happy fates awaited one-time Lincoln foes Franklin and Pierce-Arrow, as well as Reo, a producer of excellent cars with singular styling. All went under well before the Forties dawned, not for lack of merit but as victims of the era's harsh economic realities.

Franklin, the nation's only successful builder of air-cooled cars, had always made money in the Twenties. But like many others, it greeted 1930 with more optimism and models than were justified, plus new styling and a new supercharged six with individually cast cylinders and overhead valves.

The 1937 LaSalle convertible (*above*) listed at
$1350; the Packard One-Twenty four-door, $1060
(*below*). *Opposite, from top*: More '37s: Nash,
Oldsmobile Six, Packard One-Twenty.

Prices were cut to encourage sales of the similar 1931 models. It didn't work, but it was all they could do.

Franklin chassis were the basis for many custom bodies. One of the more unusual was the Pirate, a four-door convertible designed by Ray Dietrich, with concave lower-body contours that fully covered the running-boards—something everyone would have 10 years hence. Dietrich also built four-passenger speedsters with fore-shortened bodywork. Most were closed cars with permanent canvas-covered tops, but a full-convertible option was available at extra cost.

A convertible coupe was included in Franklin's new 1933 Olympic series, the firm's lowest-priced model line ever, cobbled up in a vain effort to stem mounting money losses. Powered by an L-head six *sans* supercharger, it was the product of a collaboration with Reo: basically a badge-engineered version of that outfit's latest Flying Cloud. At about $1500, the Olympic convertible was good value, well built and pretty, but it was too little too late. Olympic production barely topped 1000 units for 1933–34; convertibles amounted to fewer than 100.

Reo, founded in 1904 by Ransom E. Olds (hence the acronym), never built more than 5000 cars a year after 1931. But several of them, particularly the convertibles, rank among the most classically beautiful automobiles ever created. Styling, by the talented Amos Northup, was always formal—based on the "correct" proportions, rooted in Greek architecture, that distinguished the more memorable cars of the period. Straight eights powered a new 1931 Flying Cloud, offered on three different wheelbases; a still larger eight motivated the magnificent Royale, one of the earliest moves toward streamlining.

Inevitably, the Reo lineup was far too broad to sustain in the withering early-Thirties market. It was radically thinned by 1934 as the firm tried desperately to economize, though convertibles would persist for one more year. Still, the Flying Clouds, even the late shorter-wheelbase models, were truly beautiful, and the 135-inch-wheelbase Custom Eight convertible was as handsome a car as America built in these years. Reo ceased car production in September 1936, though it survived as a truckmaker for another 40 years.

Convertible sedans and roadster-coupes were seen from Pierce-Arrow, another fine marque that died during the Depression. After several lean years, the firm regained its independence from Studebaker in 1933, emerging healthier than its erstwhile guardian. A new board of directors thought Pierce could break even at 3000 units a year and make a million dollars at 4000. But the respected stalwart built only 2152 cars during 1933, fewer than under Studebaker.

From there, it was all downhill despite a restyled, more streamlined array of 1934 models that paid homage to Phil Wright's daring '33 Silver Arrow show car. After little change for '35, the line was fully redesigned again, becoming more fashionably rounded still. Briefly, in 1936, it seemed Pierce had turned the corner, but sales soon tapered off again and production was suspended in 1937. A 1938 lineup was announced, but only 30 cars were registered by the end of that year.

Throughout this trying period, Pierce offered about as many open body styles as anyone. Among its 1934–35 Eights and 1936 models were "convertible roadster-coupes" seating just two passengers in utter glory on huge wheelbases. But production was

Opposite page: The 1937 Packard Twelve (*top*) rode a 139-inch wheelbase, delivered 175 bhp. The '37 Pontiac DeLuxe Eight convertible sedan (*bottom*) had a two-inch-longer wheelbase, 75 fewer horses.
This page, from top: The 1938 Buick Century went for $1359, and 694 were built. Meantime, only 58 examples of the '38 Cadillac Series Seventy-Five convertible sedan found homes. The Series Seventy-Five convertible coupe listed at a lofty $3380. More affordable, a '38 Ford DeLuxe convertible sedan started at an even $900 and 2743 buyers choose one. It had a 112-inch wheelbase and the V-8 delivered 85 bhp.

Clockwise from top left: Some '38s: Packard Eight,
$1365; Chevy Master, $755 (2787 built); Lincoln
Zephyr, $1700 (600 built); Plymouth DeLuxe, $850
(1900 built), Hudson DeLuxe Eight, $1121.

THE CADILLAC-FLEETWOOD CONVERTIBLE SEDAN
[with trunk]

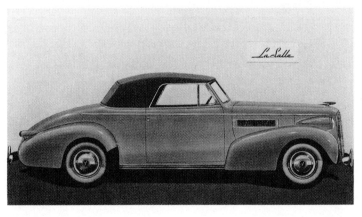

La Salle

This page, clockwise from top: The '38 Nash Ambassador Six had a 121-inch wheelbase, 105 bhp, and listed at $1099. Ragtops from GM: '39 Buick Special, $1077 (4809 built); '39 LaSalle Series 50, $1395 (1056 built); '39 Cadillac Fleetwood, $3945 (36 built); '37 Oldsmobile Eight, $1080 (728 built). *Opposite page*: Two 1939 Ford convertibles: DeLuxe coupe, $788, and DeLuxe sedan, $921. Output was 10,422 and 3561.

the lowest imaginable. In 1937, for example, Pierce completed only 121 eight-cylinder cars in all, and just a handful were convertibles. That year's Twelves numbered only 71, with open styles totaling fewer than 10.

It is sad to recall the Depression's toll on such famous makes, if only because so many had distinguished histories and impressive cars. And the list goes on: Marmon, which never built a bad car and produced in its waning years of 1931–33 what many consider one of the best ever, the fabled Sixteen; Jordan, whose Playboy roadster had helped revolutionize car advertising; Peerless, another terminally ill veteran that sought to recover with a V-16, only to expire before it could reach production. All offered convertibles: Marmon its Eights and Sixteens (1930–33), Jordan its mid-range Eights (1930–31), Peerless its Standard and Master Eights (1930–31; only one

Peerless Sixteen was built, a Murphy sedan). A shame they had to die well before the Depression bottomed out.

But ironically, the automotive design developments of 1940–1975 would be almost wholly the result of lessons learned during the Thirties. If the Depression meant the end for some companies, it forced the survivors to think, plan and invent. In so doing, they literally altered the shape of the automobile's future. Not until the fuel crises

The 1939 Plymouth DeLuxe two-door convertible
(*above*) sold for $895 and 5976 were built. The
four-door (*below*) cost $1150; output reached 387.
Opposite page: Two competitors: 1939 Lincoln
Zephyr V-12, $1839; Packard One Twenty, $1700.

and market upheavals of the 1970s would American cars be so dramatically transformed.

Likewise, the Thirties saw open body styles change from "regular" models to the epitome of devil-may-care playfulness. One by one in 1929–30, then with a rush in 1931–34, the major manufacturers switched from old-fashioned roadsters and tourings to genuine convertibles—coupes and sedans with convenient folding tops and roll-up glass windows. Gradually, convertible top mechanisms acquired power assistance: hydraulic at first (as early as 1939), later electric. Meanwhile, the convertible coupe handily outgunned the costlier convertible sedan in popularity.

The Thirties, then, was the era when the convertible acquired its modern image as a car for a limited but necessary market, designed as the ultimate sporty style among production bodies. Both trends would continue in the Forties, though they'd be interrupted by war and stalled a bit afterwards by an even more practical development: the *hardtop* convertible.

CHAPTER THREE:
1940~1949

The Race to Produce

In spring 1940, as the Nazi Blitzkrieg tore through the Low Countries and France, America and its auto industry were enjoying what was proclaimed as a generation of peace. But President Roosevelt, faced with isolationist sentiment in many quarters, promised that the nation would not go to war even as he worked to involve her at first opportunity. It was the kind of political duplicity that would make big headlines 35 years later. In the Forties, though, we were all on the same side.

Despite a shortage of skilled workers as defense needs began syphoning them off, 1940 was a good year for the U.S. auto industry. People rushed to buy (concluding perhaps that the peace wouldn't last), taking close to 3.3 million cars, a 50-percent gain over 1939. The following year's volume was higher still—a record 4.3 million cars—but by the last day of 1941 the country had been at war three weeks. Civilian car production ended by government order two months later; it wouldn't resume for nearly four years.

Historically, 1941 marks the beginning of the "standard-size" American car, the land cruiser that in a decade would be larger than anything built anywhere else in the world. In horsepower, from Willys to the heaviest Cadillacs, the trend was up. Chrysler products were redesigned and enlarged. Packard fielded the Clipper—longer, lower and more streamlined than previous models. Studebakers were wider. Hudsons had longer wheelbases.

Convertibles sold well in a market swollen by the demands of a national economy revived by war work. About 160,000 were built in 1940–42—nearly 100,000 in 1941 alone, when soft-tops garnered a respectable 2.7-percent market share. Industry ranks had been sadly depleted, however. Big Three aside, the only automakers still around were independents American Bantam, Graham-Paige, Hudson, Hupp, Nash, Packard, Studebaker and Willys-Overland.

With 141 bhp from its straight eight, the Century
was Buick's performance model in 1940. The soft
top listed at $1343, but only 550 were built.

Willys, then under the spirited leadership of saleswise Joe Frazer, launched a new 1940 line invoking patriotism, the Americar, but there were no convertibles. Ditto for Studebaker, Hupp and G-P. The last two, barely alive, would leave the auto business by 1941.

American Bantam of Butler, Pennsylvania, would disappear too, but not before building its only convertible: the cute little Riviera. The Bantam had appeared in 1936 as an evolution of the American Austin (a license-built version of Britain's cheap and cheery Austin Seven) and was always offered as two- and/or four-passenger roadsters. The Riviera was more civilized and stylish, designed by Alex Tremulis (who'd go on to create the Tucker and many handsome designs for Kaiser-Frazer and Ford in the postwar period). Tremulis recalls that a Riviera would cruise at 75-80 miles an hour and average 42.5 miles per gallon—"but not at the same time!"

Forties Bantams were powered by a 20-horsepower, 50-cubic-inch four-cylinder engine (up from 13 bhp and 46 cid) in a simple chassis spanning a petite 75-inch wheelbase. The Riviera was the prettiest model, but Americans weren't quite ready for tiny cars of any kind and the firm was almost broke by 1939, when it built just 1229 vehicles. While turning out fewer than

The 1940 Cadillac Series Sixty-Two convertible (*top*) was Cadillac's cheapest at $1795, yet only 200 were built. It was powered by a 135-bhp V-8. The Special was Buick's "bargain basement" convertible in 1940 (*far left*), listing at $1077. At that price, output reached 3763 units, seven times more than for the Century, which cost $250 dollars more and had 34 more horses. Chevrolet's convertible was part of the top-line Special DeLuxe series for 1940 (*left*). It carried a price tag of $898 and found 11,820 eager buyers.

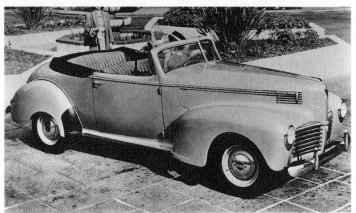

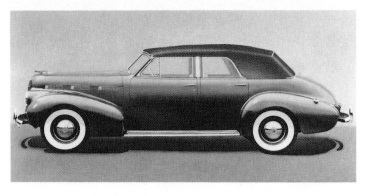

1000 cars in 1940–41, Bantam sought salvation in the Army's new general-purpose-vehicle project, supplying the first acceptable prototype for what became the Jeep. It later turned entirely to building Jeeps, but the Army needed them faster than Bantam could deliver, and the firm went under once its contract was canceled.

Before proceeding further, we should note that the convertible sedan disappeared from the American scene after 1942, not to return until Kaiser-Frazer's cobbled-up afterthought of 1949. The following chart conveys just how peripheral open four-doors had become by 1940—and how rare they are today.

Obviously, General Motors was the only one of the majors who really bothered with "convertible phaetons" after 1939. Buick offered one in each of its five 1940 series, then deleted all but

Convertible Sedan Production 1940–42

	1940	1941	1942
Buick	0	834	0
Cadillac	122	400	0
LaSalle	200	—	—
Mercury	200[1]	0	0
Oldsmobile	0	119	0
Packard	300[1]	343[2]	0
Total	822	1696	0

[1] author's estimate
[2] total based on highest surviving serial numbers

the Super and Roadmaster versions for '41 (though special-order styles on the top-line Limited chassis were still cataloged, most executed by Brunn). Oldsmobile, meantime, belatedly fielded its first and only convertible sedans, both top-liners: a Series 90 for 1940 ($1570), a Custom Cruiser 8 (Series 98) for '41 ($1575).

LaSalle breathed its last in 1940, the only year when Cadillac's companion make offered two model lines. These were beautiful cars and somewhat scarce, none more than the ragtops. The junior Series 50 saw just 599 convertible coupes and 125 convertible sedans; respective figures for the plusher Series 52 Special were 425 and a mere 75. Cadillac then stepped up production of its Series 62 convertible sedan and priced it $230 below the 1940 version (of which only 75 were built). The result hardly seemed worth the effort, though: a paltry 400 for the entire 1941 model year.

America's only other late-prewar convertible sedans came from Mercury (1940) and Packard (1940–41). The 1940 Mercurys, which also included three closed sedans and a convertible coupe, were lovely, with rounded, prow-front styling by the

Chrysler ragtop prices started out at $1160 for 1940 (*top left*). Convertibles for '41 (*far left center, and to the right*): Ford DeLuxe, Hudson Eight, Mercury Eight, Nash Ambassador, Lincoln Continental, LaSalle Special, Oldsmobile four- and two-door Series 90 Custom Cruisers.

talented Bob Gregorie. The Packards were far more opulent; those with bodies designed by Howard A. "Dutch" Darrin were possibly the most beautiful four-door convertibles ever built.

Darrin's Packard connection stemmed from his 1937 decision to return from Paris to Hollywood, where he set up a studio to create exotic adaptations of production cars for movieland society. His first such Packard was a convertible coupe on a 1938 Eight chassis for singer-actor Dick Powell; he did another 16-18 similar customs in 1938-39. With these, Dutch convinced Packard to add three Darrins to its 1940 catalog: convertible victoria (coupe), convertible sedan and four-door sport sedan.

While Dutch had previously worked on the One Twenty chassis, Packard insisted that these "production" Darrins be Super Eights (Series One Eighty) for prestige reasons. The sport sedan was quickly dropped, so most Darrin Packards were convertible victorias. Only five '40s and one '41 were convertible sedans, but they were the best of the lot. As Warren Fitzgerald wrote, "They had the long 138-inch wheelbase, combined with the three-inch longer hood, which made for stunning proportions." Stunning prices, too: around $4600 for the two-door, an imposing $6300 for the four-door.

But Packard's traditional place as America's luxury leader was in jeopardy by then. While the medium-price One Twenty and Six had been essential during the Depression, they left the firm heavily oriented toward volume models. After the war, when it could have resumed building nothing but luxury cars, Packard continued down its prewar path and would ultimately be wiped out by Big Three competition.

The 1940-42 Packard lines abounded with convertible coupes and sedans, starting with the $1100 One Ten two-door. Though four-door converts were dropped after '41, two-doors were retained, as were their older, four-square bodies. The all-new '41 Clipper sedan, the first envelope-body Packard, met with great acclaim, but the war precluded a convertible derivative (though there would have been one otherwise by 1943).

Packard would get around to a Clipper-based ragtop, but not until the un-

Opposite page: Only a few 1940 Packard Darrin convertible sedans were built (*top*). The '41 Chevy Special DeLuxe ragtop (*bottom*) was more popular—15,295 were built. *This page, from top:* The '41 Chrysler New Yorker sported clean styling and a Highlander interior option. The '41 Cadillac Series Sixty-Two featured lots of chrome

fortunate "pregnant elephant" restyle of 1948. By that point, the felt lack of a convertible was so acute that Packard released the Super Eight version six months before the rest of the line. Despite a shortish, 120-inch wheelbase, it was an impressive-looking car for the day, and relatively popular: 7763 were sold at $3250 each. Far more lavish was that year's Custom Eight ($4295), riding the 127-inch chassis and carefully crafted inside and out. Counting 1105 Custom Eights, Packard was the largest producer of luxury convertibles that year—for the first and last time after the war. From 1949 on, Cadillac's lone soft-top would outsell all of Packard's by four to one.

The only other convertibles from independent producers in 1940 were Nashes and Hudsons. All were fine examples of the two-door breed, with fresh, contemporary styling and hand-buffed leather upholstery. Confusingly, Hudson retained the term "convertible sedan" for its more lavishly equipped 1940 soft-tops and all its 1941–42s, though none had four doors. "Sedans" were identical in size and seating with convertible coupes but cost more, partly because of detachable rear side windows that gave them a different top-up appearance

(coupe tops had blind quarters). Both styles were available for 1940 as a DeLuxe Six, Super Six, and Eight.

Hudson's 1941 convertibles were engineered to be as solid and durable as its sedans (rare among period ragtops), with a specially designed, heavily reinforced frame for the first time. Hudson also offered its first power top, controlled by a dashboard button. Rear side windows were now standard but no longer detachable, lowering with the top instead. Offerings comprised DeLuxe and Super Sixes and Commodore Six and Eight (the last three on 121-inch wheelbases, versus the DeLuxe's 116). All continued for 1942.

Hudson produced about 1000 convertibles a year in 1940–41, far fewer in abbreviated model year '42. Unlike Packard, however, Hudson had planned well for convertibles and was thus able to offer them again immediately after the war, though 1946–47 choices were limited to Super Six and Commodore Eight.

Nash, like Hudson, had fully restyled for 1939. Its '40 facelift was similar, with a pointed nose carrying a slim vertical grille between chromed "catwalks" inboard of the headlamps. Nash switched to unit construction for 1941 but retained a separate body/

chassis Ambassador convertible (called "All-Purpose cabriolet") in limited production for that year only. The model didn't surface again until 1948 when 1000 were built—Nash's last large ragtops.

From here on, the story is mainly one of convertible coupes. Detroit's foremost builder of them by the Forties was not Ford or Chevrolet but Buick, which had long stressed open styles and usually sold a larger percentage than rival makes. For example, Buick built 18,569 of its '41 convertible two-doors—one model each in the Special, Super and Roadmaster series—the highest count for any nameplate between 1937 and 1947. At just over $1000, the Special accounted for about half the annual totals. Buick had a banner '41 overall, producing 374,000 cars.

Like most everyone else, Buick warmed over its 1942 models as stopgaps for the first three years after the war, but the Special convertible and Century series didn't return. Relying strictly on $2000-$3000 Super and Roadmaster two-doors, Buick continued with the industry's highest convertible volume: 8600 in 1946, 40,000 in 1947, 30,000 in 1948. The big topless Roadmaster, with its huge chrome

66

Opposite page, *clockwise from left*: A few 1941 convertibles: DeSoto Custom, $1240, 2937 built; Ford Super Deluxe, $946, 30,240 built; Lincoln Zephyr, $1858, 725 built. *This page*: Two elegant '41s, even with tops up: Lincoln Continental (*above*) and Packard One Twenty (*below*).

teeth and phallic hood ornament, became a symbol of predicted peacetime prosperity, likely coveted by more Americans than anything else on wheels in 1946–47. Cadillacs, after all, were pricey; Buicks were more attainable.

Yet not all Forties Cadillacs were expensive. Once LaSalle departed, Cadillac spread down into the upper region of LaSalle's former price territory. One result was that a 1941–42 Sixty-Two convertible coupe could be had for under $2000. But perhaps people didn't realize this, because the ragtop didn't sell: only 3608 went out the door during 1940–42. Postwar, it was a different story: 1342 of the '46s, 6755 of the '47s. The Sixty-Two was the only Caddy convertible to survive the war, but then it was the only one needed.

In GM's mid-price ranks, Olds and Pontiac worked hard at ragtops prewar, selling 11,000 of their '41s combined. Neither make listed fewer than two models, usually split between the top and bottom series. The Pontiacs cost about $1000; the '41 Oldsmobiles ranged from a $1048 six-cylinder 66 to the $1227 eight-cylinder 98 version. Both makes fielded similar offerings postwar, albeit at higher, inflation-fueled prices. The Olds 98 became one of GM's first new postwar cars with its mid-1948 "Futuramic" redesign, but no convertibles were immediately available. The old 98 remained popular, though. It accounted for about three-fourths of the make's 1948 convertible sales, which totaled close to 17,000, making Olds number three in soft-tops behind Buick and Chevy. (Pontiac, at 16,000, ranked fourth.)

Chevy convertibles finally began outselling Ford's in 1940, when new "Royal Clipper" styling made for a thoroughly more attractive car than Chevy had built for some time. (Not inaccurately, some still describe it as a mini-Cadillac or Buick.) Chevrolet achieved this success with just one top-line convertible selling at $800-$1000 (a Special DeLuxe for 1940–41, a Fleetmaster for 1942–48) and continued its lead after the war except 1946. With its plodding "Stovebolt" six, a Chevy convertible couldn't keep pace with an open Ford V-8, but at least it looked better.

Ford and Mercury were restyled for 1941, but neither was an improvement and it cost: for the model year, Ford built only 700,000 cars while Chevy

Opposite page: Plymouth built 10,545 Special DeLuxe convertibles for 1941 (*top*) at a retail price of $1007. The '42 Buick Roadmaster (*bottom*) was a bit pricier at $1675, and rarer with only 511 built. *This page*: More '42s: Lincoln Zephyr, $2150, 191 built; Mercury Eight, $1215; Chevrolet Fleetmaster, $1080, 1182 built.

The war was finally over! Automakers trotted out slightly warmed over '42s as 1946 models, among them (*clockwise from top left*): Mercury Sportsman Eight, $2209; DeSoto Custom, $1761; Pontiac Torpedo, Six or Eight, $1631 and $1658; Dodge Custom, $1871; Plymouth Special DeLuxe, $1439.

topped the million mark for the first time. The advent of an L-head Ford Six didn't help, though it was also offered as a convertible. Again like most others, both Dearborn makes relied on warmed-over '42s for 1946 to 1948, but added luster to the lines with new limited-production convertibles: the wood-bodied Ford and Mercury Sportsmans.

Developed from Bob Gregorie's wartime styling sketches, the 1946–48 Ford and 1946 Mercury Sportsmans featured white ash and mahogany on doors, rear fenders and deck (structural around the aft quarters). It was an attractive way to freshen up the old

styling, and it boosted showroom traffic. But the Sportsmans weren't cheap: $1982-$2282 for the Ford, $2209 for the Merc—about $500 upstream of their all-steel counterparts. Production thus ran to only 3485 Fords and just 205 Mercs. Glamorous convertibles were arguably best left to Lincoln.

And glamorous they were. Model year 1940 brought one of the decade's most stunning cars: the Zephyr-based Continental, an Edsel Ford idea executed by Bob Gregorie. Rakish long-hood/ short-deck proportions, Dearborn's then-favored prow front, outside spare tire and a sleek yet "formal" roofline

made it "thoroughly continental" per Edsel's instructions. A closed coupe and wide-quarters cabriolet were offered at $2850 each, and they lured customers into dealerships by the thousands (some of whom went away in one of the less-expensive Zephyrs, which still included a shapely convertible two-door). The '41 Continental, split off from the Zephyr line, enjoyed slightly higher volume.

For 1942, all Lincolns acquired a more reliable, 305-cid version of the flathead Zephyr V-12, plus a flashy facelift with higher, squared-up fenders, reduced ride height and chromier, more complex grillework. The last was

One of the most memorable of all Chryslers surfaced in 1946: the wood-trimmed Town & Country, a sleek wagon prewar, now an elegant closed sedan and convertible coupe. The topless T&C, beloved of Hollywooders from Tyrone Power to Leo Carrillo, was the better seller and more successful than Ford's Sportsmans, with over 8500 built through early 1949.

The T&C's white ash trim was sheer hell to maintain, but this wasn't much of a problem for the moneyed, new-car-every-year folks able to afford such rigs, and heaven knew we needed interesting cars in 1946-47. The last T&C ragtops of 1949 sold for $3900, which was more than most Cadillacs, while all-steel Windsor and New Yorker convertibles soldiered on at $2000-$2500. While it lasted, the T&C was good publicity.

Led by upstart newcomer Kaiser-Frazer, Detroit's first all-new postwar designs began appearing in 1946, though because of an unprecedented seller's market, most would be held back to model year '49. K-F, of course, had it easy, having built no cars prewar and thus having no dies to amortize. Predictably, its initial entries were sedans (bearing smooth, slab-sided Dutch Darrin styling). Convertibles would have to wait.

This left Studebaker to release the industry's first new postwar soft-tops: the 1947 Regal Deluxe Champion ($1902) and Commander ($2236), of which 6000 were built by January 1948. The 112-inch-wheelbase Champion was on the stubby side, but the Commander looked very good indeed, a tribute to the radical new styling by Virgil Exner of the Raymond Loewy team.

Most other makes apparently considered convertible coupes important enough to include as part of their new postwar fleets. Only those of Oldsmobile, Nash and Kaiser-Frazer didn't have one, and each was a special case. K-F was new, but would shortly go topless. Nash elected to build no large convertibles after '48. Olds introduced its new-design postwar models in two stages: the 98 as a mid-1948 entry, the 76 and 88 as '49s—by which time each had a convertible, 98 included.

Hudson and Kaiser-Frazer built the most unorthodox early-postwar soft-tops. The former debuted its famous "Step-down" cars for 1948, with smooth, low lines and unitized con-

This page: 1947 Buick (*top*) was America's convertible king: 40,371 built. Hudson produced about 1500 Super Six ragtops (*center*). Pontiac fielded sixes and eights for 1948 (*above*), but the cheapest drop top now cost over $2000. *Opposite*: Studebaker, here a '47 (*top*), was "First by far with a postwar car!" Ford turned out only 3459 Sportsman ragtops for 1946-47 (*bottom*).

Lincoln ended the Continental Mark I series in
1948 (*above*) with output of 452 cabriolets.
Opposite, clockwise from top: Three new postwar
designs: '49 Ford Custom, '48 Olds "Futuramic"
Ninety-Eight, '49 Buick Super. Nash built 1000
'48 Ambassador Customs, its last full-size ragtop.

struction of granitic strength. Among them were no fewer than three convertibles, more than any other manufacturer: Super Six and Commodore Six/Eight. Called "brougham" (thus reviving pre-1940 nomenclature), they bore a broad steel header above the windshield. Hudson claimed superior roll-over protection, but former chief engineer Stuart Baits told this writer that it was a matter of economics. The header was simply a remnant of decapitating the closed two-door body to eliminate the need for separate convertible dies.

Kaiser-Frazer's convertible, announced for 1949, was unique for its day in having four doors. Production economies were at work here, too, because a four-door sedan was all K-F had bodywise. Like Hudson's, its convertible's header was carved from a sedan roof, leaving a small but noticeable expanse of steel.

Unfortunately, the prototype K-F

convertible lacked the structural integrity of Hudson ragtops. As engineer Ralph Isbrandt remembered: "It was like a bowl of jelly... You couldn't see out the rearview mirror on a smooth road. We finally convinced management that GM, Ford and Chrysler weren't putting X-member frames and special pillars on convertibles for the fun of it, and then we began to get results... but the frames alone cost us $600 each. They were not only 'X'd' but reinforced all over hell. Every time we could find another patch we would slap it on."

When body engineer John Widman pointed out that the convertible needed structural B-pillars, stylist A.B. "Buzz" Grisinger came up with vertical glass panels framed in chromed metal to provide the necessary reinforcement without disrupting the body lines. It was a makeshift arrangement at best. Neither the little panes nor the chrome side-window frames

were removable or retractable, remaining in place with the top up or down. It was all just a funny exercise, as only 124 of the '49s were assembled: about 66 Kaisers and 46 Frazers. A handful were reserialed as 1950 models.

Ford and Chrysler entered 1949 with all-new designs across the board, and GM completed its postwar overhaul with like updates for Chevy, Pontiac, Buick and the junior Oldsmobiles. (The Olds 98, as mentioned, and all Cadillacs save limos were redesigned for '48.) Ford and GM adopted much sleeker lines on full-envelope bodies; Chrysler persisted with bolt-on rear fenders and a more upright stance.

GM's styling was arguably the best—inspired, according to design chief Harley Earl, by the wartime Lockheed P-38 pursuit fighter aircraft. Every make wore smooth, flowing bodywork and, Chevy excepted, distinctive hallmarks. Pontiac had "Silver

Streaks," Buick "ventiports," Oldsmobile rocket insignia (denoting the division's new high-compression overhead-valve V-8), and Cadillac (which had its own new short-stroke V-8 that year) tailfins and massive eggcrate grilles.

Buick, once a cornucopia of convertibles, canceled its Super but produced over 30,000 Special and Roadmaster models—massive, brightly decorated cars selling respectively for about $2100 and $3100 and riding 121/126-inch wheelbases. Chevy did even better with 32,932 examples of its sole convertible, in the Styleline Deluxe series, a neat little car still well liked today. Cadillac continued with its soli-

tary Series 62 ragtop, of which 8000 were sold at $3442. Pontiac and Oldsmobile, spanning a broader price spread, cataloged five convertibles between them. Olds served up three, ranging from $2148 (in the six-cylinder 76 series, fast waning in sales) to $2973 (the big 98, the most popular at 12,602 units). The Pontiacs were all deluxe-trim models in the Chieftain Six and Eight series, tagged at around $2200.

But Ford had America's favorite 1949 convertible, wresting the sales lead from Chevy on the strength of its fine new postwar design by Dick Caleal of the George Walker organization. Offered only as a Custom V-8, the

soft-top accounted for 51,133 units, the highest of any Ford convertible yet. Lincoln and Mercury were also rebodied for '49, becoming large, bulbous "bathtub" styles—distinctive if not exactly pretty (though arguably more so than Nash's similar attempt). Lincoln had two soft-tops, standard and Cosmopolitan, costing $3200/$4000 and produced sparingly: only 743 for the calendar year. Mercury's single entry, priced at a more attractive $2416, brought 16,765 sales, another record.

Had there been styling awards in '49, Chrysler Corporation would have received the "Most Underwhelming" trophy. As ever, this company was

Opposite page: The '49 Cadillac had a new 160-bhp V-8 (*top*). The '48 Chrysler Town and Country (*bottom*) sported wood bodysides and a $3395 pricetag. *This page*: The all-new '49 DeSoto (*above*) saw output of 3385 Custom ragtops. The '49 Frazer Manhattan four-door soft top (*below*) listed at $3295—only 70 were built for 1949-50.

Six convertibles for 1949 (*this page*, *clockwise from top*): Hudson Commodore Six, $2952; Mercury Eight, $2410; Pontiac Chieftain Eight, $2206; Lincoln Cosmopolitan, $3948; Lincoln, $3116.
Opposite page: Packard built 1237 Super Eights for 1949 at a list price of $3250 each.

The 1958 Buick was often criticized for having its chrome put on with a trowel. Perhaps, but this Buick Limited was smooth, quiet and powerful.

Most cars for 1950 bore only mild facelifts, but
sales set a record that year, and the ragtops
looked as desirable as ever. Seen here: Mercury
(*above*), Oldsmobile 88 (*below*), Hudson Commodore
(*right*), and the Ford Custom (*right bottom*).

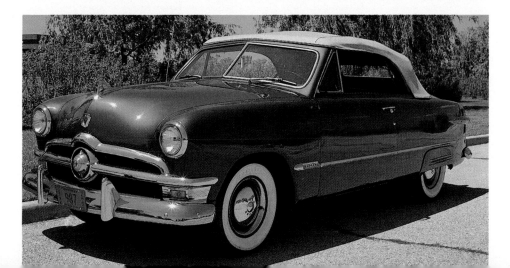

Ford made it a genuine convertible with roll-down windows and gave it a bolt-on hardtop for wintertime comfort (Corvette acquired these for '56). The Vette body was fiberglass, the T-Bird's conventional steel. Early Corvettes had six-cylinder engines; the T-Bird bowed with a burly Mercury V-8, part of the new overhead-valve family that first appeared in Fords for '54. Also unlike the early Corvettes, manual transmissions were available. The Bird did race, but it was really a "boulevard sports car."

The concept worked: For debut '55, Ford's two-seater outsold Chevy's 24:1. But the rivalry ended almost as soon as it began. Corvette was transformed into a genuine sports car—and a convertible—for '56, while the Thunderbird became a four-seater—and a hardtop—after 1957. But the convertible remained, accounting for one of every seven T-Birds sold in 1959.

If the Thunderbird was romantic, Ford's 1957–59 retractable-hardtop Skyliner was exotic. Employing a feature proposed for the Mark II Continental, it was the only mass-market convertible of its kind (though not the first: Peugeot had one in its 1936 Eclipse, and Chrysler's 1940 Thunderbolt show car was a "retrac" too). It seemed like a good idea at the time, and Ford made a legitimate point by asking, "How can it be a 'hardtop *convertible*' if the top doesn't go down?" But as a typically Fifties idea, the Skyliner proved a complicated beast with lots to go wrong.

Sharing Ford's all-new '57 platform, the biggest ever, the Skyliner had a huge steel roof that disappeared into a high, wide rear deck via a bevy of servo motors and miles of wiring. Even then, the top had to have a hinged front flap to fit, and left precious little trunk space when stowed. The "retrac" was expensive, too: over $400 more than the soft-top Sunliner (both offered only in top-line Fairlane 500 trim). That combined with mechanical problems to turn off customers, and production went from 20,766 for model year '57 to 14,713 for '58, then to 12,915 for '59, after which the Skyliner was abandoned (at the bidding of division chief Robert S. McNamara) as a superfluous gimmick.

Other unique retrac features included a V-8 as standard (extra-cost on Sunliners from '55), relocated fuel

Clockwise from top: The 1950 Pontiac Chieftain
DeLuxe listed at $2190. Cadillac produced 6117
Series Sixty-Two convertibles for 1951, compared
to 3854 Olds Super 88s, about 550 Hudson Hornets,
and 857 Lincoln Cosmopolitans. *Opposite page*:
Frazer built only 131 ragtops in 1951.

tank (behind the back seat instead of under the trunk floor) and foreshortened greenhouse. Like other Fords, the Skyliner was heavily restyled and re-engineered for 1959. At mid-year it became part of the new top-line Galaxie series, though it still wore Fairlane 500 script. More fascinating than ever today, the Skyliner remains a monument to a time when Detroit thought it could do anything.

Mercury had nothing so radical, and no two-seat sports cars, but convertibles played a role in its Fifties fortunes. For 1952 it reverted from 1949-51's "small Lincoln" to its original status as a "big Ford," then reached peak sales in 1955-57 with over 10,000 soft-tops a year, making it seventh in convertibles after Ford and the five GM divisions. There was only one Mercury convertible through mid-decade, always in the most expensive series (Monterey for 1952-54, Montclair for '55). Beginning with the '56s, certain Mercury hardtops were called "Phaetons," though they were nothing of the sort.

That same year, Mercury began moving into Ford country with the low-price Medalist series and added a less costly convertible to the step-up Custom line, priced at $2712 (versus

$2900 for the soft-top Montclair). Mid-model-year '57 brought a third convertible, a roofless version of the glitzy Turnpike Cruiser.

Billed as a "dramatic expression of dream car design," the Turnpike Cruiser was conceived mainly as a topline hardtop coupe and sedan. Both shared 1957's new Mercury-only body/chassis and jazzy styling, but stood apart with "skylight dual curve" windshield, reverse-slant roofline with drop-down backlight, dual air intakes atop the A-pillars (housing little radio antennae no less) and "Seat-O-Matic," an embryonic memory seat that assumed one of 49 preset positions at the twist of a dial. Only the last was found on the Convertible Cruiser, which arrived as a replica (complete with owner-applied decals) of the one that paced that year's Indianapolis 500.

Despite a raft of gimcracks including pushbutton Merc-O-Matic transmission—or perhaps because of them—only about 16,000 of the '57 Cruisers were built, of which 1265 were convertibles. The soft-top vanished for 1958, when Turnpike Cruiser applied only to hardtops in a Montclair subseries. The name was then consigned to the scrap heap as Mercury reverted to a three-series line with two convert-

ibles, base Monterey and top-echelon Park Lane.

Lincoln's more dignified clients were habitually offered one convertible through the Fifties. The big, bulbous 1950-51 Cosmopolitans, with their curious "sad-eye" faces, saw very few copies (536 and 837, respectively). Cosmo was demoted to junior status for '52 and Capri came in to head the line, the ragtop remaining in the upper series. Convertible Capris saw somewhat higher volume than Cosmos but were no match for Cadillac; 2377 of the '53s was the best they'd ever do. Capri then moved down to make room for Premiere as the premium version of the wildly restyled, lower-longer-wider 1956 design; again, the convertible stayed in the senior series. Lincoln sold 2447 soft-tops that year and 3676 of the '57s, the latter a record for the decade.

With dreams of rivaling GM as a multi-division producer, Ford formed a separate Continental Division to sell the $10,000 Mark II hardtop of 1956-57, then decided its impressive ultra-luxury car cost too much to build for what it brought in corporate prestige and showroom traffic. When Lincoln switched to a huge all-new unibody design for 1958, four Mark III derivatives were fielded as top-line models, though at much lower prices than the Mark II. Lincoln's convertible transferred to this line and sold at $6283; only 3048 were built. For 1959, Continental was folded back into a reconstituted Lincoln-Mercury Division and officially became a Lincoln again. That year's $7056 Mark IV convertible saw but 2195 copies.

Lincoln's best Fifties convertibles undoubtedly came in the 1952–54 "Road Race" years, when Lincoln built some of America's most roadworthy cars and dominated the Mexican Road Races. These Lincolns also happened to be gracefully styled and beautifully put together. Then Lincoln went wild with tailfins, slant-eyed fronts and the "extruded look," losing quality as well as good taste. But that seemed to be exactly what the public wanted: 1957 and '58 were Lincoln's best convertible years.

Which brings us to Edsel, Ford Motor Company's ill-starred attempt at a second medium-price make. Though the very name has since become synonymous with "loser," Edsel wasn't nearly the failure people imagine it was. It cost Ford anywhere from $100 to $250 million—not exactly a drop in the bucket for even a big company, but no occasion for bankruptcy either—and it was not entirely unsalable: 50,000 units wasn't bad in the recession of '58, Edsel's first model year.

Granted, Ford had planned for much more, invested heavily in plants and dealerships, and initially fielded no fewer than four Edsel series on three different wheelbases. There were two convertibles: the $3200 Pacer, a close cousin to that year's Ford, riding a 118-inch wheelbase; and the $4000 Citation, a Mercury relative on a 124-inch chassis. Both had gadgets galore, like "Teletouch" automatic transmission controlled by pushbuttons buried in the steering wheel hub, a surprisingly poor location. The Citation carried a jumbo 410-cid V-8 with 345 horsepower and was quite impressive at its price. But Edsel convertible output was ridiculously low: 1876 Pacers, 930 Citations.

The 1959 Edsel line was drastically trimmed and all models made more like Fords. There was only one convertible, in the upper-series Corsair group, on a middling 120-inch wheelbase; 1343 were built. Edsel died soon

This page, from top: More convertibles for 1951: Lincoln Cosmopolitan, $3891; Chevrolet DeLuxe Styleline, $2030, one of 20,172 built; Kaiser prototype, which unfortunately never went into production. *Opposite page*: The $3391 Packard ragtop (*top*) was built on the 122-inch-wheelbase 250 series. Mercury (*bottom*) charged $2380 for a '51 convertible and built 6759 of them.

after the '60 models were announced. Again there was but one ragtop, in the remnant Ranger series. Production was a mere 76. The Edsel name was considered for the uplevel Ford Falcon compact that became the Mercury Comet, but had already become the butt of too many jokes. The automotive namesake of Henry Ford's brilliant son deserved a better fate. (At least the name may gain a more positive image now that Edsel Ford II, son of late company chairman Henry Ford II, has been named to the Dearborn board of directors.)

Though Ford Division was the dominant make in Fifties convertible sales, General Motors was the decade's big gun in corporate convertible volume. Four of its brands—Chevrolet and the B-O-P nameplates—usually ran 2-5, and even Cadillac was no slouch, averaging about 10,000 topless cars a year.

Cadillac built some of GM's most interesting Fifties convertibles, certainly the most expensive. Through 1952, the division continued with a single Series 62 model that tallied about 6500 units a year. For 1953, Cadillac added the Motorama-inspired Eldorado, essentially a 62 with custom interior, cut-down "Panoramic" wrapped wind-

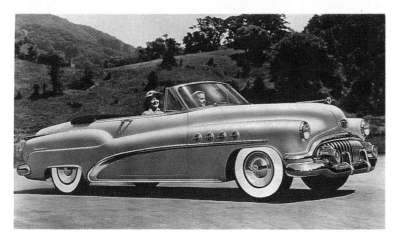

shield, distinctive notched beltline, and a metal instead of canvas cover for the stowed top. The Eldo wasn't intended to make a profit—and at $7750 and only 532 units, the '53 didn't—but rather to bring in customers for the ordinary models, which it did.

But when Cadillac restyled for '54, the game plan changed. Cut $2000 in price, the Eldorado went all out for sales: 2150 found buyers that year,

thus establishing the model as a limited-production money-spinner. By 1955, Eldorados wore their own special "shark-fin" rear fenderlines; a year later came an Eldorado Seville hardtop to match the convertible, now called Biarritz.

Eldorados were technically part of the Series 62 until 1959, when they were broken out as a separate group. Combined, the Eldo and Series 62 put

Cadillac convertible volume into five figures for the first time in 1955, a level that was usually maintained in subsequent years. The Eldo was heroically overdecorated next to the 62, glistening with chrome and $2000 dearer. But though never intended for high volume, it did account for up to 20 percent of Cadillac's convertible production—quite good, all things considered.

Clockwise from top left: The effects of the Korean conflict meant lower production and higher prices in 1952: Chevrolet DeLuxe Styleline, $2128; Mercury Monterey, $2370; Pontiac DeLuxe Chieftain, $2444 and $2518; Hudson Hornet, $3342; all-new Lincoln Capri, $3665; and Buick Roadmaster, $3453.

In convertibles as most other matters, Cadillac outdid Lincoln as well as Packard, once a rival to both makes but fated to a sad death in the Fifties. Until the 1952 arrival of James Nance as company president, Packard had built convertibles almost as afterthoughts: a handful of dumpy Supers and Customs in 1950, then a series of short-wheelbase 250s on the junior (Clipper) body for 1951–53. The latter were nice, well built and reliable—and utterly boring. At $3400–$3500, they were more competitive with Buick and Chrysler than Cadillac.

Setting out to recapture past glories, Nance asked stylist Dick Teague to create a limited-edition soft-top for 1953. The result was the Caribbean, with handsome, clean-limbed open-wheel styling and a 180-bhp straight eight. At $5210, it was $2500 cheaper than the Eldo and thus handily outsold it. But Packard hit the skids in 1954, planning to bring out a new line but settling for a facelift. Only 400 of the '54 Caribbeans and 863 conventional convertibles were sold, all still with the junior body on its relatively short chassis.

But Nance got his big restyle for '55, including a lavish new Caribbean on the long wheelbase at last. It was Packard's only soft-top that year, priced at $6000. Historians say it was another traffic-builder never intended to make money, though it's hard to imagine Jim Nance okaying anything without profits in mind.

Packard had a fair year in 1955 but fell apart in 1956. Customers deserted what they perceived was a failing brand and dealers bailed out in favor of Big Three franchises while the factory nursed quality control and production problems. The '56 Caribbean was a fabulous car, and its reversible seat cushion covers (leather on one side, cloth the other) were a novel touch, but just 276 were built. Even then, there were leftovers.

Packard hastened its decline by purchasing Studebaker in 1954, a bad piece of business. Having absorbed most of Packard's remaining capital and good will, Studebaker became the dominant partner, and the 1957–58 Packards were just glorified Studebakers. We can be glad there were no convertibles among them—and sad for the end of a great marque.

Returning to General Motors, we find a vast range of convertibles in the

Fun under a 1953 sun (*clockwise from above*): Buick Super, $3002; Cadillac Series Sixty-Two, $4144; Chevrolet Bel Air, $2175; Ford Crestline Sunliner, $2043; Cadillac Eldorado, $7750. Respective outputs were 6701; 8367; 24,047; 40,861; and 532. Note the Panoramic windshield on the Eldorado.

revised for postwar models, which were prewar carryovers except that the 292-cid engine returned and the "Zephyr" name didn't. The Continental reached a yearly production peak in 1947 at 1569 units, only to vanish a year later (though not permanently).

Chrysler Corporation's 1940–42 convertibles were conventional and low-key, sprinkled among the various lineups wherever it was thought they'd do the most good. Chrysler offered Windsor Six and New Yorker Eight models, the former occasionally sporting vivid "Highlander plaid" or "Navajo" upholstery. Dodge and Plymouth had one apiece, slotted into their higher-price spreads. Ditto DeSoto ex-cept for 1942, when it offered Custom and Deluxe ragtops. Appropriate, per-haps, since DeSotos were more inter-esting that year, bearing "Airfoil" hidden headlamps (the first since the Cord 810/812's) and a sculpted, half-naked maiden as a new mascot. The eyelids vanished postwar, but the hood ornament persisted through '48.

Clockwise from above: More '53s: DeSoto FireDome
V-8, $3114; elegant Packard Caribbean, $5210; Ford
Sunliner, $2043; Plymouth Cranbrook, $2220; and a
'54 Hornet, the last Detroit-built Hudson, $3228.
Only 750 Caribbeans and 1700 DeSotos were built;
Plymouths were more common with 6301 produced.

popular Buick, Olds and Pontiac lines spanning the wide medium-price sector of the Fifties market. But Alfred Sloan's dictum of "a GM car for every price and pocketbook," was now turning into "a Buick, Olds and Pontiac for every price" as the three divisions went toe-to-toe, model-for-model. This would prove disastrous in the very long run: A quarter-century later, GM was saddled with multi-make dealerships selling near-identical model groups to increasingly bewildered buyers. In the Fifties, though, such intramural rivalries helped move a lot of cars.

Buick, usually the industry's leading convertible maker in the Forties, fell behind in the Fifties as Ford and Chevy volume soared. But Buick continued to place great emphasis on soft-tops. It began the decade with three, reviving a Super to complement Special and Roadmaster models, then wowed the public in 1953 with the handsome Skylark, a sort of Buick Eldorado.

The Skylark was the most successful of 1953's three limited-edition GM convertibles, seeing 1690 units compared to only 532 Eldorados and 458 Olds Fiestas. Another Harley Earl

exercise, it sported a restyled lower body with full-radius rear wheel openings, and came with every conceivable extra: whitewalls, power steering and brakes, station-seeker radio and deluxe interior. The price was equally lush: $5000. Much cleaner than the chromey standard Buicks, the Skylark was bereft of their trademark fender portholes and used wire wheels instead of wheel covers. But its '54 successor was more conventional and—with big, tack-on chrome tailfins—rather gaudy. After only 836 of these, the Skylark was retired.

No matter. Buick was destined for bigger things—notably a production surge that would take it ahead of Plymouth into third place behind Chevrolet and Ford. This was achieved in calendar year '54 and model year 1955. Reflecting its exuberance, Buick offered no fewer than five 1954 convertibles: the aforementioned Skylark, the usual Special/Super/Roadmaster trio, and one in the newly revived Century series. Prices ranged from $2563 for the Special to $3521 for the Roadmaster. Arguably most desirable was the hot-rod $2963 Century, with the big 200-horsepower 322-cubic-inch

Roadmaster V-8 in the lighter, short-wheelbase Special body. A well-tuned Century ragtop could do 0-60 mph in 10 seconds and 110 mph flat out. No wonder Buick sold about 5000 a year in 1955–57 at prices in the $3000-$3600 range.

A revised '58 Buick lineup saw the Super series trimmed and a new Limited version of the Roadmaster, priced $500 higher. Buick retained four convertibles, a Limited model replacing the previous Super, but these garish cruisers were the wrong cars for a recession year. Suddenly, a public that seemed tired of the horsepower race and acres of chrome began turning to compact Ramblers and the strange little Volkswagen. The '59 Buicks were locked up before that became apparent, but were much better cars nevertheless: smooth if flamboyant, and well engineered. They were also renamed, with convertibles in the

Clockwise from top left: Cadillac built 2150 Eldorado ragtops for 1954 at $4738 each, while Olds ran off 6800 Ninety-Eight Starfires for $3249. At $1100 less, Ford turned out 36,685 Sunliners. Nash's Metropolitan cost but $1469, a Skylark, $4483; Buick made 836 of the latter.

This page: Two '54s: the $3935 Packard (863 built)
and the $2301 Plymouth Belvedere (6900 built).
Opposite page, from top: Convertibles were "in"
during record-breaking 1955: Chevrolet Bel Air,
$2305; Cadillac Eldorado, $6286; Chrysler Windsor
DeLuxe, $3090; and the Lincoln Capri, $4072.

LeSabre, Invicta and Electra 225 series at base prices of $3200-$4200.

Oldsmobile followed a more modest convertible program, fielding a 98 and Super 88 (plain 88 for '50) through 1956 (plus 973 tail-end 76 convertibles in 1950). The aforementioned '53 Fiesta, a semi-show car in the 98 line, was priced too high to sell ($5717) and vanished after just one year.

After zooming to fourth in the industry by 1955, Olds confidently launched a restyled line of 1957 "Golden Rockets" that included 88, Super 88 and 98 convertibles. All continued through 1959 and notched combined output of up to 22,000 a year.

Pontiac, too, was far more flush by mid-decade, moving from its traditional sixth to the number-five slot. Through 1953 it cataloged two softtops: a Six and Eight on identical wheelbases. The Six finished up in '54 and a new straight-eight Star Chief series arrived with that year's only Pontiac convertible. Things would stay this way until 1958, when a second ragtop, in the baseline Chieftain series, was added. But it was nothing like still a third drop-top Poncho, the Bonneville.

When Semon E. "Bunkie" Knudsen became Pontiac general manager in 1956, he set out to alter the make's rather staid image. The Bonneville, introduced as a mid-year '57 model, was one of the ways he did it. Pontiac had adopted a modern V-8 for '55. The Bonnie had the latest 347-cid version and packed 300 bhp via fuel injection, hydraulic lifters and racing cam. It made for the fastest Pontiac yet—faster still with optional Tri-Power (three two-barrel carbs), able to leap the quarter-mile in 16.8 seconds. A $6000 price made for only 630 sales in the first year, but a newly styled and more affordable '58 ($3586) sold 3096. For 1959, still sharing bodyshells with Chevrolet but with its own distinctive styling, Pontiac made Bonneville its new top-line series, adding a wagon and hardtop sedan to the previous convertible and hardtop coupe. The drop-top sold over 11,000.

Against V-8 Fords, Chevrolet had always had an uphill battle for convertible sales. As noted, its 1950–54 line of good-looking but low-powered six-cylinder cars never approached Ford's volume. But things began to change with the '55s: the best Chevys yet and, as many agree, some of the best

American cars ever built. They also ushered in Chevy's first modern V-8, the excellent 265 small-block, shepherded into production by chief engineer Ed Cole.

Suddenly, "Chevrolet" meant "performance," and a Bel Air convertible was the hottest low-price car around. No surprise, as the '55 Ford was a heavily facelifted '54, while the '55 Chevy was all-new, beautifully styled, built with care and available in a raft of colors (including handsome two-tones). It only got better through the deft Cadillac-like restyles of 1956 and '57. We can see how this high-powered soft-top—transformed for '58 into an even more deluxe Impala model—altered the score by looking at the model year production figures:

The Impala was one of the bright spots in a generally dismal 1958. Chevrolet built 181,000 of them (more than Ford built Edsels) despite just two body styles, convertible and hardtop coupe. They were arguably the best expression of Chevy's determined move up-market, with '58's larger, heavier body and big new 348-cid V-8. Fuel injection, which got more publicity than it deserved, had arrived as a '57 option, but high price meant few passenger Chevys were so equipped. Luxury was the key in the Impala class, and Impala succeeded. Like Pontiac did with its Bonneville, Chevy added pillared and pillarless Impala sedans to form a new top-line 1959 series. All four body styles, convertible included, were available with six or V-8. Chevy's '59 styling will ever be criticized, but its convertibles still outsold Ford's!

Meantime, the Chevy Corvette had gone from sales chump to sports-car champ, partly by adopting convertible features. They first appeared on the '56s, along with curvy new styling that completely did away with the former "bathtub" look. The '57s were outwardly unchanged but went faster, thanks to that year's enlarged, 283-cid small-block and optional fuel injection that offered up to a like number of horses. Handling improved too. A bulkier, weightier body with four

Wraparound windshields, V-8s, and flashy two-tones were big selling features in 1955. Seen here (*clockwise from top left*) are the DeSoto Fireflite, Pontiac Star Chief, Ford Thunderbird, Cadillac Eldorado, Packard Caribbean, Oldsmobile 88, and (*in the center*) the Plymouth Belvedere.

Low-Price-Three Convertible Production 1950–59										
	1950	**1951**	**1952**	**1953**	**1954**	**1955**	**1956**	**1957**	**1958**	**1959**
Ford	50,299	40,934	22,534	40,861	36,685	66,121	73,778	119,882	51,876	69,044
Chevrolet	32,810	20,172	11,975	29,664	19,383	41,292	44,735	53,901	65,157	82,435
Plymouth	12,697	9,500	6,150	6,301	6,900	8,473	6,735	9,866	9,941	11,053

The '56s were mainly facelifted '55s, but convertibles remained popular (*above and clockwise*): Chevrolet Bel Air, $2344; Lincoln Premiere, $4747; Pontiac Star Chief DeLuxe, $2857; Mercury Custom, $2712; and Buick Super, $3544.

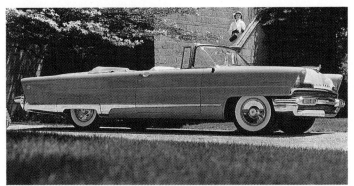

Most '57s were all new—longer, lower, wider and costlier. Among the ragtops were (*above and clockwise*) the Cadillac Eldorado Biarritz, $7286; DeSoto Firedome, $3361; Imperial Crown, $5598; Oldsmobile Super 88, $3447; Buick Super, $3981.

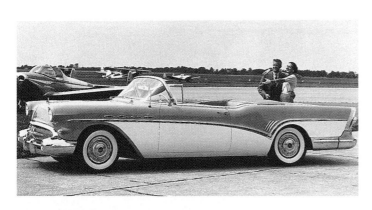

Clockwise from top left: Chevrolet was facelifted for 1957, and had 283 horsepower with fuel injection. Chrysler's legendary 300-C had 390. The '57 Ford Thunderbird had 300 horses with supercharger, and sported modest fins that looked like those on its bigger brother, the Fairlane 500. The all-new Dodge, here a Coronet, had unique fins, which it referred to as "Swept Wing."

headlamps and more chrome made the '58 aesthetically less pleasing, but performance wasn't affected and volume went up. The '59s were treated to a minor cleanup and tallied 9670 units, a long way from the 3467 Corvettes built for '56. Chevy's sports car was here to stay.

The foregoing production chart shows how badly Plymouth trailed in convertibles, not only behind the Big Two but the other GM makes and Mercury. Despite a vigorous sales recovery on the strength of its stylish '55s and their new V-8 engines, Chrysler's breadwinner usually ran seventh in convertible volume. One reason: a hard-to-shake conservative image. In this, Plymouth was even worse off than Chevrolet, which could boast more dealers and a "best-seller" tradition.

Plymouth rode a roller coaster in the Fifties. After Detroit's dullest '49 restyle, its 1950–52 models were little different and their 1953–54 revisions weren't much better. The '55 was something else, though: shapely, colorful and eye catching, the work of Maury Baldwin and Virgil Exner. Plymouth was all-new again just two years later—the style leader of the Low-Price Three—and its V-8s were at least a match for the competition's. But soft-top sales didn't budge, perhaps because the ragtop got no emphasis. Even Plymouth's hottest, the 1956–58 Fury, came only as a hardtop coupe.

Through 1958, Plymouth offered only one convertible, in the top-line series as usual: Special Deluxe (1950), Cranbrook (1951–53), Belvedere (1954–58). With such low volume, it made sense to standardize the V-8 for '55. The '57s were dramatic-looking and very impressive, the convertible wearing a special compound-curve windshield wrapped up at the top as well as around to the sides.

A second Plymouth convertible arrived for 1959 as a companion for that year's new Sport Fury hardtop, with up to 305 horsepower from a ram-induction 361-cid "Golden Commando" V-8. Big and flashy, the Sport Fury was what convertible buyers wanted and claimed over half of Plymouth's ragtop output that year, which itself was the highest since 1950.

Dodge was equally dull in the early Fifties but more interesting than Plymouth, thanks to several unique

models. One bowed with the new low-price Wayfarer series of 1949: an open three-seater with side curtains, which was thus technically a roadster. For 1950 it acquired roll-up windows to become a convertible, and looked more "important." Sales were never significant: 2903 of the '50s, 1002 of the similar '51s.

The standard Dodge convertible of these years was always in the premium Coronet series, which received the new "Red Ram" 241 V-8 for 1953. The name changed to Royal for '54, when 2000 were built. Included were 701 Royal 500s, hot machines in the image of that year's Indianapolis pace car, supplied with chrome wire wheels, continental spare tire, special badges and a 150-bhp Red Ram. Dealers could even specify a four-barrel Offenhauser manifold that made this somewhat dumpy drop-top a genuine scorcher.

With a snazzy 1955 facelift, Dodge, like Plymouth, became a serious competitor again. From 1956 through 1959 there were always two convertibles, Coronet and Custom Royal—three if we count 1957's new D-500 option, available on any model in the line. This gave you firm suspension, a 245-bhp

hemi V-8 and 0-60-mph times of around nine seconds. The bold and rapid D-500 continued for 1958-59, though a wedgehead engine replaced the hemi. Offered with fuel injection for 1958, the 361-cid wedge produced 333 bhp, a new Dodge high.

Though DeSoto had some of its best sales years in the Fifties, its place in the Highland Park hierarchy was being steadily undermined by Dodge from below and Chrysler from above. DeSoto enjoyed record volume in 1955, almost outproduced Chrysler in '57—and was gone by late 1960.

DeSoto persisted with one upper-echelon convertible through 1954, then expanded in a big way: a Fireflite and Firedome for '55, a special Fireflite Pacesetter for mid-'56 (100 replicas of that year's Indy pacer), a new Adventurer model for '57, and four different soft-tops—Firesweep, Firedome, Fireflite, Adventurer—for 1958-59. Then . . . nothing, as DeSoto was left with a truncated line of sedans and hardtops for 1960-61.

The wildest DeSotos were the pre-1960 Adventurers, limited-production jobs with arresting color combina-

Opposite page: A Mercury Turnpike Cruiser (top), labeled "Convertible Cruiser," paced the '57 Indy 500. Ads for the '57 Plymouth, here a Belvedere, boasted, "Suddenly its 1960!" This page: Pontiac debuted the Bonneville in 1957 (above). The '58 Buick Limited was two inches longer than a Caddy.

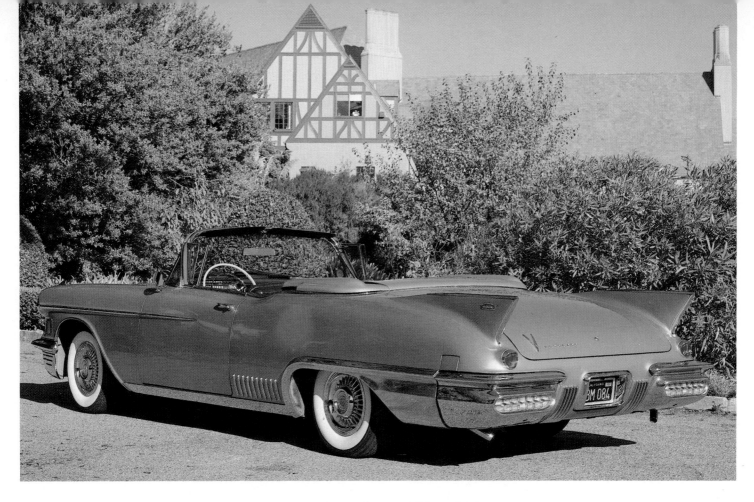

Clockwise from above: The '58 Eldorado Biarritz
sported unique rear-end styling. The '58 DeSoto
Firesweep ragtop sold for $3219, the Imperial
Crown for $5729. The Ford Fairlane 500 Skyliner
retractable hardtop, at $3163, cost $500 more than
the Sunliner; the Chevy Impala listed at $2841.

tions, acres of anodized aluminum trim and the hairiest engines (in '57, for instance, a 345-cid hemi with one bhp per cubic inch). Convertible production was very limited: 300 of the '57s, 82 for '58, and just 97 of the '59s—now collector's items all. They could fly, too: fast-shifting TorqueFlite automatic took most Adventurers from 0 to 60 mph in around seven seconds and on to 125 mph or more. Torsion-bar front suspension gave these big bruisers surprisingly good handling.

Lesser DeSoto ragtops were hardly more numerous. In fact, the highest production for any V-8 DeSoto convertible came with the 1956 Fireflite: just 1385. Others are counted in the hundreds.

Chrysler Corporation is a leading convertible-maker today. But as the foregoing makes clear, its soft-top business was peripheral in the Fifties. This was true even for the high-priced Chrysler and Imperial, which had always done well with ragtops. Chrysler consistently offered two models— Windsor and New Yorker—through 1956, plus an Imperial version for '51, but annual volume was measured in four small figures. It remained so for 1957, when the soft-top Windsor was replaced by the first convertible 300, a muscle car of impeccable breeding.

The '57 Chryslers were among Virgil Exner's best designs—gracefully finned and beautifully clean—though nobody knew then how quickly they could rust. Hemi V-8s and torsion-bar front suspension made them among the most roadable cars in America.

The 300C convertible, with up to 390 bhp, high-grade interior and unique frontal styling, listed at $5359 (close to $6000 delivered); just 484 were built. The following year's 300D notched up only 191 convertible sales, and 1959's wedgehead 300E scored but 140. The New Yorker, slightly less lavish but more affordable ($4600-$4900), fared little better: for 1957–59 respectively, 1049, 666, and 286.

Imperial became a separate make for 1955 but wasn't offered as a convertible until 1957. That happened to be Imperial's best year ever, the only one in which it would outsell Lincoln. Helping were 1167 Crown convertibles at $5568 apiece. From then on, the soft-top languished at 500-700 units a year as one ornate facelift succeeded another. The convertibles were

Counterclockwise from top left: The '58 Edsel,
here a Pacer, was a sales flop, but it didn't look
any worse than a lavender '58 Oldsmobile. The
Pontiac Bonneville was all-new for 1958, as was
the Lincoln Continental Mark III, the latter
sometimes called a "land barge." The 1959
Chevrolet, shown in Impala form, grew huge "bat
fins" and sported unusual "nostrils"
above the grille.

as big and impressive as any Imperial but, despite heroic efforts, never cut heavily into Cadillac sales, the highest among domestic luxury convertibles. One problem was price: The Crown cost several hundred dollars more than a Cadillac 62, which had a more prestigious name and better resale value.

The Fifties were disastrous for all the independents. Packard's fate has already been mentioned. Partner Studebaker almost died with it, but was rescued at the eleventh hour (in 1958) by Curtiss-Wright, mainly as a tax-loss.

Car companies tend to cut back when the going gets tough, but Studebaker had cut out convertibles well before its mid-decade crisis. Its only Fifties soft-tops were thus the little Raymond Loewy Champions and somewhat larger Commanders of 1950-52. The Commander received a fine new V-8 for 1951, which gave its convertible real performance. What it needed was real styling. Studey was still plying its basic 1947 design, made bizarre with the "bullet-nose" facelift of 1950-51, more acceptable with the "clam-digger" front of 1952 (the firm's centennial year). Relative to its size, Studebaker sold a fair number of convertibles. A shame it never found the money to produce an open version of the beautiful 1953 Starliner coupe, though that wouldn't have helped stave off the inevitable.

Nash built no large convertibles after 1948, but did produce a popular little one: the six-cylinder Rambler, which arrived in 1950 and was also offered as a two-door station wagon. Though its window frames were fixed and only the top dropped, the roofless Rambler won people over—perhaps because, at $1808, it was 1950's cheapest convertible. A total of 9330 were built for the model year. The convertible remained in production through 1954 and was always competitive; its price was up to only $1980 by then. As an economy car, it had no performance, of course, and its unit body was a devilish ruster. Still, America's first modern "compact" was pleasant as a convertible and, in its way, unique.

Arriving in 1954 to succeed Nash's small convertible was an even smaller one: the three-passenger Metropolitan, which also came as a coupe. Built in England with an Austin engine but resolutely Nash in appearance, the petite 85-inch-wheelbase Met enjoyed its

greatest popularity in 1959 when over 22,000 were sold, about a third of them soft-tops.

A few Metropolitans were also badged as Hudsons. It's unclear when the last of these were sold, but the car simply became "Metropolitan" once Nash and Hudson expired in '57. Technically then, this was Hudson's last convertible. The big ones had ended in 1954. The last recorded production for Hudson soft-tops is 1952, when it listed 636.

All this is strange in a way, because Hudson seemed a strong proponent of convertibles. For 1950 it had no fewer than five: Pacemaker and Pacemaker Deluxe on a new 119-inch wheelbase; Super Six and Commodore Six/Eight on the familiar 124. The line was rearranged for 1951 and the potent Hornet arrived; it, too, was offered as a convertible, called "Brougham" (as were all drop-top Hudsons in this period). Even

in 1953–54, the last years for "real" Hudsons, soft-top Wasps and Hornets remained available.

Hudson probably offered so many convertibles because they were so easy to build, sharing many body panels with sedans and coupes. Engines, wheelbases, badges and trim were shuffled to produce the various permutations. All remained true to the original 1948 "Step-down" design, with strong unibody construction and

More '59 convertibles from Detroit (*clockwise from top left*): Buick Electra 225, $4192; Oldsmobile Ninety-Eight, $4366; Plymouth Sport Fury, $3125; Pontiac Catalina, $3080; Ford Thunderbird, $3979; and the Chrysler 300-E, $5749. Of the six, the 300-E ragtop was easily the rarest of the lot with only 140 built.

that massive windshield header. And the Hornet, at least, was impressively quick—at 112-115 mph, America's fastest six-cylinder car. A pity more ragtops weren't built.

Willys-Overland brought out its first new car in a decade in 1952, but the handsome little Aero didn't come as a soft-top (evidently because it had unit construction too). No sooner had it appeared than Willys was swallowed by what was left of Kaiser-Frazer,

which wasn't much.

The last of K-F's unique convertible sedans were offered as 1951 Frazer Manhattans. These were basically left-over 1950 Kaisers and Frazers "restyled" with new front and rear ends. Surveys of survivors suggest original production of between 128 and 131. Why so few? A high price—$3075—and a face only their mother could love.

As for Kaiser, its second-generation

design for 1951 was all-new and beautiful, again the work of the artistic Dutch Darrin. Convertibles were mooted and one prototype was actually built, but the company would never have the funds to get one into production. Ditto hardtops, station wagons and V-8s. These deficits, plus Henry Kaiser's intransigence and the money-sapping Henry J compact, culminated in 1955 with the departure of Kaiser-Willys from the U.S. car market.

Chutes
and Ladders

Cadillac started out the Sixties by lowering its
1959 fins and cleaning up the styling. The
Eldorado Biarritz convertible retailed for $7401.

The events of the Sixties are probably more responsible than those of any other decade for where we are today. All of us who were above the age of 10 or so in 1963 remember where we were on November 22, the day we all died a little. Every time we see a rocking chair or a game of touch football, we stand a chance of being reminded of it. Somehow, life was never quite the same afterward.

For Detroit, the Sixties was the greatest decade yet. Nineteen sixty-five saw a new yearly production record that would not be surpassed until 1974; 1966 and 1969 were almost as good, and annual volume was never under seven million cars after 1962.

The Sixties were also the best years for American convertibles. Over half a millon were built in '65, a record that will probably never be equaled, let alone topped. Their heyday was 1962–66, when ragtops enjoyed a six-percent market share, up from only 4.5 percent in 1960.

Yet in the end, the Sixties was a giant game of Chutes and Ladders: By 1969, the convertible's market penetration had been cut by half. A few years later, soft-top models would account for less than one percent of all Detroit cars.

The Sixties convertible leaders were remarkably constant. With one exception, the top five producers were always the same: Chevrolet, Ford, Pontiac, Buick and Oldsmobile, which finished in that order in five of the 10 model years. The exception was 1961, when Cadillac built a few more convertibles than Olds. In 1965–66, largely on the strength of its popular new Mustang, Ford managed to build more soft-tops than Chevy. Once the "ponycar" craze subsided, though, Chevrolet was again the convertible leader, and in 1968–69, Pontiac ran second, ahead of Ford.

Independents were hardly in the convertible business during the Sixties, mainly because there were hardly any independents left. Let's begin with their story.

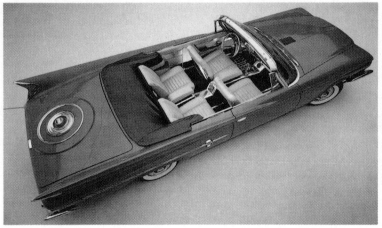

Studebaker-Packard (renamed Studebaker Corporation in 1962) returned to convertibles for 1960 with a compact Lark offering, its first soft-top in eight years. At 8571 units, model year production was rather good, considering the South Bend automaker hadn't built more than that many convertibles a year since 1950. But the pace wouldn't last. Regarding Studebaker's and Rambler's initial success with compacts, this author always likes to paraphrase automotive writer Rich Taylor: Independents are sometimes capable of stealing a march on giant manufacturers, but before they know it, they have elephant footprints all over them.

Styled by Duncan McRae, the pert

and practical Lark was a clever, shortened and reskinned update of Studebaker's old 1953-58 sedan/wagon platform (several years of huge deficits precluded an all-new design). It arrived for 1959, when people were turning away from Detroit dinosaurs and toward imports like the seemingly preposterous Volkswagen. Big Three compacts were then a year off, so Studebaker shared the domestic small-car market only with Rambler, which was doing even better. People who wouldn't have been caught dead in a Studebaker showroom a year earlier scrambled to buy Larks in '59. Calendar year production rose from 45,000 in 1958 to over 126,000, and Studebaker made an unaccustomed profit.

The Lark was a good product, available with Studebaker's old L-head six or its somewhat younger—and still spunky—259 V-8. From the first, Studebaker wisely offered several body styles: two-door wagon, hardtop coupe and two- and four-door sedans. The new-for-'60 convertible came only in upmarket Regal trim at starting prices of $2600-$2700. The '61 version was little changed apart from slightly squarer contours.

Unfortunately, neither the convertible nor the Lark line as a whole could maintain their strong initial sales. Between formidable rivalry from the Falcon/Corvair/Valiant trio and certain problems of its own, Studebaker could only watch its sales plunge. For 1964,

114

Clockwise from top left: Ragtops for 1960: Chevy Impala, $2954; Edsel Ranger, $3000; Oldsmobile Super 88, $3592; Ford Galaxie Sunliner, $2860; Chrysler 300-F, $5841; Buick Electra 225, $4192. The Edsel, now in its last year, and the 300-F are particularly rare, as only 76 and 248 units, respectively, were produced for the model year.

the last year of domestically built Studebakers, total production was only 37,000. Aside from an elderly basic design (and despite Brooks Stevens' nice facelifts for 1962 and '64), the Lark was saddled by its inherited tendency to rust badly and fall apart. Because of this and Studebaker's increasingly publicized corporate troubles, resale values declined steadily each year. Then too, South Bend's dealer force was weak, and growing weaker.

For 1962, Studebaker added a bucket-seat V-8 convertible called Daytona, then put the label on all its '63 ragtops. But by then, the Big Three compacts all had convertibles too, and each undercut the Daytona's price. Studey convertible volume thus hovered around 2000 units for 1961–62, dropped to 1000 for '63, then only 703 of the '64s, all V-8 Daytonas. Convertibles—and a good many other models—were dropped for 1965–66, when the firm departed South Bend and consolidated operations at its Canadian plant in Hamilton, Ontario. After that, Studebaker abandoned cars altogether. Though convertible ver-

Clockwise from top left: Plymouth Fury kept its high-flying fins for 1960, while the Lark Regal was Studebaker's first soft-top since '52. The "wide track" Pontiac Bonneville sold for $3476 in 1960, the restyled '61 Chevy Impala, $2954; the Dodge Dart Phoenix, $2988. It took $3382 to drive the all-new '61 Buick LeSabre ragtop home.

sions of the sporty Hawk and glamorous Avanti coupes were contemplated, they never went beyond the drawing board.

Rambler enjoyed much higher volume and a much better public image than Studebaker, George Romney's American Motors surprising just about everybody—including Romney—in the late Fifties. By 1960, Rambler was fourth in overall volume at well over 400,000 cars. In 1961 it displaced Plymouth as number three, then built a record 428,346 cars in 1963 (though that was good for only eighth in the industry that year).

Romney, who thought only of compacts, stepped aside as AMC president and chairman in 1962. New president Roy Abernethy looked at the company's volume and decided it meant that AMC should go toe-to-toe with the Big Three in every market sector. AMC tried, but only bloodied its nose—badly. This wasn't entirely Abernethy's fault, as AMC dealers were demanding a broader range of cars. At any rate, AMC's mid- to late-Sixties offerings—American, Ambassador, Marlin, Javelin, Classic, Rebel and AMX—were ambitious but still not enough to compete fully with the much greater expansions of Chevrolet, Ford, Pontiac and others. By 1969, its last year as a separate make, Rambler ranked 10th in industry volume at 250,000 units; other models grouped under the AMC marque accounted for about 175,000 more.

Rambler's sole convertible for 1961–63 was a 100-inch-wheelbase American model, attractively tagged at around $2400 base. The original 1958 American was a resurrected, slightly restyled 1953–55 Nash Rambler, a recession-market emergency measure. The '61 was simply a reskinned version, styled by craggy AMC chief designer Edmund Anderson so as to keep the old design going a few more years. A new convertible and hardtop coupe were part of the plan. But aesthetically, it didn't work, the cars looking very boxy and truncated. One English designer hired by AMC compared them to ordnance vehicles.

Nevertheless, the American convertible turned a profit, recording 13,497 sales for '62 (the only year for which we could find sales figures). Far more efficient than expiring Studebaker, AMC was able to build this convertible to a price competitive with those of Valiant, Falcon and Corvair models. That was the key to its success—along with the parent company's hearty reputation at the time.

Completely restyled by Dick Teague on a six-inch longer wheelbase, the '64 added good styling to the American's list of attributes. Though bucket-seat hardtops had been available for a couple of years, the convertible continued in the mid-range bench-seat 440 series, priced at $2346.

With the convertible suddenly a serious salesmaker for the first time in anyone's memory, AMC decided to add Classic and Ambassador soft-tops for '65. Both lines were cleanly restyled that year, and the latter was stretched to 116 inches between wheel centers, 200 inches overall (a size that would have been anathema to Romney). AMC called its '65s the "Sensible Spectaculars," but convertible sales weren't rousing: 12,334 for the three models combined.

Ambassador was officially a Rambler series through 1965, then registered as a separate AMC "make." Otherwise, the company's '66 convertibles were the same: one American, one Classic, one Ambassador. Classic became a Rebel for '67, and along with Ambassador acquired smooth new "coke-bottle" styling, one of Teague's best (and still underappreciated) efforts. Responding to the era's sporty-car craze, the American convertible became a bucket-seat Rogue ($2600 base) that year and the former

Classic 770 was similarly transformed into a Rebel SST ($2800). The '67 drop-top Ambassador appeared in the lush, top-line DPL series ($3143).

Only the Rebel remained for 1968 (when that name achieved make status too), though a base-series 550 convertible arrived ($2736), perhaps to make up for the loss of the American. Respective production was just 377 and 823 units. These would be AMC's last convertibles until the soft-top Renault Alliance of 17 years later. The Rambler marque itself ended after 1969, by which time AMC was switching to new names like Matador and Gremlin, all registered as "makes."

Turning to the Big Three, Chrysler (the make) never seemed able to sustain its previous soft-top success in the Sixties. Indeed, the production record suggests that those who've glommed onto certain offerings had better keep them; there probably aren't that many left. Consider, for example, the following:

Selected Chrysler Convertible Production 1960–68

Year	Model	Production
1960	300F	248
1961	New Yorker	576
1961	300G	337
1962	300H	123
1964	300K	625
1965	300L	440
1968	300 Sportsgrain	175

Clockwise from top left: The '61 Chrysler New Yorker convertible retailed for $4592; only 576 were built. Two luxury ragtops for 1961: Imperial Crown, $5774, 429 built; Lincoln four-door, $6713, 2857 built. The all-new '61 Ford Thunderbird convertible listed at $4639, compared to $2849 for the heavily facelifted '61 Ford Galaxie Sunliner.

Clockwise from above: Monterey was Mercury's top-line '61 series; 7053 ragtops were built. The '61 Pontiac Bonneville sold for $3476. Lincoln built America's only four-door convertible in the Sixties, while Oldsmobile entered the personal-luxury market in 1961 with the $4647 Starfire.

The letter-series 300 never made any money. Perhaps it was never expected to, even after bean-counters replaced enthusiasts in Highland Park's executive suites. But the 300 did achieve its objective of establishing Chrysler as a builder of hairy-chested performance cars, albeit large ones.

In those days, Chrysler sniffed snobbishly at compact-toting competitors like Buick and Mercury, proudly announcing, "There will never be a small Chrysler." Minds would change later on, but it was a good sales ploy at

the time. In fact, contemporary market conditions didn't really warrant a small Chrysler, since Chrysler dealers also carried Plymouth, which had many smaller models—*too* many, in fact.

All the letter-series 300s were memorable, none more than the convertibles, available each year from 1957 through '65 except 1963. Big and bucket-seated, packed with power and style, they could show a clean pair of heels to most anything on the road and do it right off the showroom floor. The original '55 C-300 had been built to

make Chrysler stock-car champion, which it did until automakers agreed to stop emphasizing speed and cease competition sponsorship in 1957. After that, the letter-series became a sort of *ne plus ultra*. Though it never ran up many sales, it remained an important "floor-traffic builder" for Chrysler dealers.

Alas, the letter-series became rather tame toward the end, much closer to ordinary Chryslers in appearance, features and performance. Then again, 1962's mighty 300H could be had with

405 horsepower, enough to blow off most any rival. And on its firm, race-bred suspension it could embarrass many a foreign sports car.

Cast in the letter-series image was a standard 300 series that replaced the mid-range Windsor for 1962. Engines were smaller and bucket seats cost extra, but prices were much lower and styling a dead ringer for that of the letter cars. These 300s were more successful, though not a lot. The most numerous of the convertibles were the '63s: about 3400 units, including 1861 specially trimmed "Pace Setter" models. The series hung around through 1971, always interesting and always with a convertible except in that final season.

Worth mentioning because of its novel looks and popularity among today's collectors is the "Sportsgrain" option for the 1968 300s: a swathe of wagon-like pseudo-wood trim along the bodysides intended to invoke the spirit, if not the "real-tree" honesty, of the Forties Town & Country. While nearly 1000 hardtops had this treatment, it was applied to only 175 convertibles. Both are now worth about twice as much as their unadorned counterparts.

Besides the non-letter 300s, Chrysler offered a low-line convertible throughout the Sixties: a Windsor for 1960, a Newport thereafter. When the non-letter arrived, the long-running New Yorker convertible was dropped. It had never sold well, New Yorker buyers evidently preferring closed models.

Of course, Chrysler-Plymouth dealers had the even bigger Imperial convertibles to sell in these years, but they didn't sell many:

Imperial Convertible Production By Model Year

1960 618	1961 429	1962 554
1963 531	1964 922	1965 633
1966 514	1967 577	1968 474
1969 0		

These flashy land yachts invariably appeared in the Crown series, a step up from the base Custom through 1963, the standard Imperial series thereafter. Styling for 1960–63 was by Virgil Exner, his fetish for Classic-era design themes apparent in big open wheel wells and, for 1961–63, free-standing headlamps encased in mas-

sive, chrome-plated shells. The 1964–66 cars were penned by Exner's successor, Elwood Engel, who brought in a Lincoln Continental touch from his work at Ford: squarish bodies with straight-through fenderlines capped with bright metal. Unlike other Chrysler products, Imperial retained a separate body and chassis until 1967, when production economics dictated a switch to unit construction. With that, Imperial increasingly became less distinctive and more a glorified Chrysler. Convertibles were the most expensive Imps short of the plush LeBaron hardtops and rarified Crown Imperial limos, selling well into the $6000-$7000 range—which at least partly accounts for their low volume.

Chrysler's junior divisions, Dodge and Plymouth, were minor leaguers in the Sixties convertible field, though the advent of compact Dart and Valiant models for '63 gave them much more soft-top business than they'd have had otherwise. The main reason is that sales of both makes' breadwinning full-size cars were greatly hampered through 1964. The 1960–61s were just too ugly to find much favor, while the 1962–64s were too small, the result of an Exner decision made long before the public was ready for "downsizing."

Opposite page, from top: Buick debuted the compact Skylark convertible for '62; it listed at $3012. The new Chevy II Nova 400 ragtop was cheaper: $2475. Compare that to the $5588 it took to buy a '62 Cadillac Sixty-Two. *This page:* For $127 less, one could buy a Chrysler 300-H, but only 123 people did so. The downsized '62 Dodge lineup included the $3268 Polara 500 soft-top. Ford gave the '62s a neat restyle. The Galaxie 500 Sunliner listed at $2924, a sportier XL, $3518. With racing in mind, a fastback top called Starlift was devised for the convertible. NASCAR banned it; few were made.

123

This page, clockwise from top: Plymouth built 1516
Sport Fury ragtops priced at $3082 in 1962. Olds
sold an F-85 Jetfire coupe, but this Jetfire
soft-top wasn't even listed in the model lineup.
More '62s: Mercury Monterey Custom, $3222, 5489
built; Lincoln Continental, $6720, 3212 built;
Ford Thunderbird, $4788, 7030 built. *Opposite
page*: Some convertibles for 1963: Cadillac
Eldorado, $6608; Chevrolet Impala, $3024; Dodge
Polara, $2963; Buick Skylark, $3011.

This involved reducing the standard Dodge and Plymouth to a 116-inch wheelbase for '62, making them 400 pounds lighter and six inches shorter than their predecessors. As automobiles, they were very good indeed, but the public rebelled at the smaller size and oddball styling, and sales plummeted. Plymouth finished eighth for the model year, a position it hadn't occupied since 1930. Dodge suffered less, partly by fielding a mid-year Chrysler-based 880 line (which effectively re-

placed recently deceased DeSoto on the corporate price ladder), then extended its "full-size" wheelbase for 1963. Thanks to more conventional styling, both makes soon recovered rapidly, emphasizing performance with 413-cubic-inch wedgehead V-8s for the street and special 426 hemis for racing (something competitors had also returned to by that point). With aluminum pistons and high-lift cam, the hemi developed up to 425 bhp, and in the light 330-series body won

Dodge the 1962 National Hot Rod Association Championship. The hemi continued to rule the strips and, beginning in 1964, the stock-car ovals.

Big Dodge convertibles for 1960–61 comprised Polara and Dart Phoenix models; 1962's were the mid-size Dart 440 and bucket-seat Polara 500, plus a big Custom 880. The Dart name replaced Lancer on Dodge's 1963 compact, which offered convertibles in mid-range 270 and bucket-seat GT trim. Priced under $3000, they were quite popular. Pushing hard at a sporty image, Dodge had no fewer than seven convertibles by 1965, its best year: the two Darts, Polara and Custom 880 models on a new 119-inch-wheelbase platform, and three in the mid-size Coronet line, a renamed, restyled '62 evolution. This broad allotment continued through the rest of the decade (and some confusing name changes).

One of Dodge's nicest Sixties ragtops was the intermediate Coronet R/T ("Road/Track") of 1967, an even livelier version of the previous year's good-looking, restyled Coronet 500. Standard equipment included bucket-seat interior, a 375-horsepower 440 V-8, heavy-duty "handling" suspension, wide tires and oversize brakes. The hemi was technically available, having been reinstated as a production option for '66, but relatively few R/Ts were so equipped.

The Plymouth convertible story mirrors Dodge's. While Dodge production totals are not largely available, it seems that Plymouth built more open cars. Plymouth's first-generation Valiant (1960–62) wasn't offered as a convertible, but when the popular compact was redesigned for 1963 (along with Dodge's), it received two: standard V200 and bucket-seat Signet.

Plymouth's finest convertibles were reserved for the Fury line: full-size for 1960–61, mid-size for 1962–64, "standard" again from 1965. Beginning with 1962, a second ragtop was offered under the revived Sport Fury name, a swashbuckling bucket-seat performer with standard V-8. Two more convertibles arrived with the intermediate Belvedere/Satellite group of 1965, riding the 116-inch wheelbase deserted by Fury. Sharing their basic engineering with the Dodge Coronet, they were good-looking cars with squarish lines, clean sides and lots of glass. The Satellite two-door convertible and hardtop were top of the Belvedere line and, like Coronet, could be ordered with a 426 V-8 developing 365 bhp and 470 lbs-ft torque, though this was a wedge, not a hemi; that engine was available only on the race-intended Belvedere Super-Stock hardtop (and Dodge's equivalent Ramcharger).

Apparently there was some moaning about this from Plymouth (and Dodge) customers, for the mighty hemi was made optionally available for selected 1966 intermediates, accompanied by oversize tires and brakes and

Clockwise from above: Ford built 18,551 Galaxie 500 XL Sunliners for 1963, compared to 15,957 Pontiac Tempest LeMans soft-tops. Olds assembled 4267 Ninety-Eight convertibles listing at $4457. Mercury turned out 5757 Comet S-22s, which started at $2710. The '64 Cadillac Eldorado Biarritz was rarer; 1870 were produced, just ahead of the 1427 Thunderbird Sports Roadsters Ford built in 1962.

H.D. suspension. First offered with a four-speed, it was later available with TorqueFlite automatic. Although it was the lighter two-door sedans and hardtop coupes that took home the dragstrip trophies, the convertible Satellite hemi was the glamor car of the line—and fast. With the right tires and axle ratio plus careful tuning, it could reach 120 mph in 12-13 seconds.

This package duly evolved into 1967's memorable Belvedere GTX, a convertible and hardtop coupe with standard 440 V-8 (hemi optional), silver-and-black grille and rear-deck appliqué, simulated hood air intakes, sport striping, dual exhausts and buckets-and-console cabin. GTXs weren't cheap—$3500 base, around $4300 with typical options—but they were elegant muscle cars, among the best of that breed.

Of course, performance lovers aren't always wealthy, but Plymouth had a muscle car for them too: the whimsical Road Runner. Arriving for 1968 as pillared and pillarless coupes, it was basically a no-frills GTX—really stark inside and out. But Plymouth didn't skimp on the good stuff: a standard 383 V-8, firm suspension, heavy-duty manual transmission. The Runner did a lot for Plymouth in the burgeoning youth market, but inevitably became plusher and costlier, beginning with the '69s. Among the upgrades was a new $3313 RR convertible that sold 2128 copies for the model year compared to over 82,000 coupes and hardtops. (Dodge also fielded a "budget" muscle car that season, the Super Bee, but didn't bother with a ragtop.)

Plymouth's one other convertible in this decade arrived with the second-generation Barracuda of 1967-69. The original Barracuda was essentially a fastback Valiant hardtop, announced in mid-1965 as a sort of Plymouth answer to the Ford Mustang (it wasn't, though the two cars arrived so close together as to make many think otherwise). The second-generation 'Cuda was longer-lower-wider and quite European in appearance. Though the 383 V-8 was newly available, the lighter, higher-revving 273 small-block was a better choice for street work. Both engines could be ordered with a Formula S package comprising H.D. suspension, tachometer, Goodyear Wide-Oval tires and special badges.

This Barracuda wasn't seriously changed through '69, but it seems to

Opposite page, clockwise from top: Buick built 7850 Wildcat convertibles at $3455 in 1964. Two '64 Chevys: the new mid-size Chevelle Malibu, $2695; and the Impala, $3035. Buick's mid-size Special Skylark sold for $2834; output hit 10,225.
This page, from top: The '64 Chrysler 300 ragtop fetched $3803 and found favor with 1401 buyers. Two more '64s: Dodge Custom 880, $3264; the all-new Thunderbird, $4953; Ford built 9198 copies.

have been too late to capitalize on the ponycar craze that Mustang had uncovered overnight—and which began waning almost as quickly. Convertibles were the least salesworthy models, generating only 4228 orders for '67, 2840 for '68 and 1442 for '69. But that's the kind of volume that excites collectors, and the package itself was a good one. The convertible 'Cuda continued into 1970's bigger and bulkier new third-generation, only to disappear two years later.

Although Ford Motor Company wasn't as dominant in convertibles as it had been in the Fifties, its Sixties soft-tops included some of the most interesting cars of all time. Notable was a revival of the convertible sedan, a body style not seen since the '51 Frazer. It debuted for 1961 as one of two all-new Lincoln Continentals.

Before it came the 1960 Continental Mark V, a continuation of the 1958–59 Mark III/IV, Lincoln-Mercury's attempt at a less costly, more salable

ultra-luxury car that would actually make money. As ever, the convertible was the most expensive model apart from the limousine, base-priced at around $7000. It tallied only 2044 units.

But even as the first of these monsters was being introduced for 1958, the decision had been made to design an all-new Lincoln. When this appeared for 1961, the giant square-rigged Marks (and related standard Lincolns) were dropped. (The Mark III tag would return, however, gracing a

much smaller new 1968 personal-luxury hardtop.)

The '61 Lincoln Continental arrived in two four-door body styles: hardtop and convertible. Styling was the work of seven Ford designers who received the annual Industrial Design Institute Award for their efforts. Most agree they earned it. Though it looked unique, the Continental shared some tooling (especially around the cowl) with that year's equally new Thunderbird hardtop and convertible, thus trimming production costs for two low-volume model lines. Yet the Lincolns were big (though much smaller and lighter than the 1958–60s) while the T-Birds were two-doors on a 10-inch-shorter wheelbase. Continental styling was crisp, chiseled and elegant. Dead-on, the windows sloped inward toward the roof—the greatest "tumblehome" yet seen on an American car and one of the first uses of curved side glass in regular production.

Unlike K-F's convertible sedans, the Lincoln's side glass and window frames completely disappeared for a pure, uncluttered look. Likewise its convertible top, which stowed Ford Skyliner-style beneath a hinged rear deck via 11 relays connecting various mechanical and hydraulic linkages. Workmanship was first-rate. Customers also benefited from the industry's most thorough pre-delivery testing and a then-unprecedented two-year/24,000-mile warranty.

This Continental also evokes memo-

More convertibles for 1964 (*top row*): Ford Falcon Sprint, $2671; Ford Galaxie 500 XL, $3495; Lincoln Continental, $6938; Mercury Comet Caliente, $2636. The restyled Imperial (*left*) offered a soft-top in its Crown series for $6003. The hot Pontiac GTO (*below*) debuted in '64 listing at $3500.

ries of JFK, being chosen as the basis for a new White House limo to replace the big Lincoln Cosmopolitan of Presidents Truman and Eisenhower. The production models saw few changes through 1963. Wheelbase was stretched three inches (to 126) for '64, but the same basic styling was retained. The precisely assembled and balanced Continental V-8, a whopping 430 cubic inches, was replaced by an even smoother and more powerful 462 for '66.

As ever, though, the convertible was more indulgence than salesmaker,

never amounting to more than about 10 percent of Continental production. It thus came to an end after '67 and the lowest convertible volume for the 1964–67 design generation: only 2276 units.

Lincoln's "other half" played a supporting role in the division's Sixties convertible business. Mercury softtop production (all two-doors) peaked with the '63s: over 18,000, a record that still stands. But dealers never seemed to push convertibles very hard, nor were the cars particularly innovative. That's probably because

Mercury didn't pioneer new products the way Ford and Lincoln did; if either make succeeded with one, Mercury might get its own version some time later. Mercury was thus unable to match sales with the Buick-Olds-Pontiac trio it had originally been created to compete with. Things are different today, Mercury offering some distinctive cars all its own.

Mercury's early-Sixties big convertibles were peripheral low-volume models: a Monterey and Park Lane for 1960 (about 7500 units), a Monterey for 1961 (when series were shuffled

Top row: The '64 Lark Daytona ragtop (*left*)—
Studebaker's last convertible—listed for a modest
$2805, while Buick asked a near identical $2834
for the '65 Skylark (*right*), of which only 1181
were built. *Bottom row*: 1964 Pontiac Bonneville
"Club de Mer"; 1965 Buick Wildcat Custom, $3727;
and '65 Chevrolet Corvair Monza, $2493.

and Park Lane axed, 7000 built), a Monterey Custom for '62 (around 5500). A "1962½" entry was the Monterey Custom S-55, priced $500 above the standard convertible ($3738) and much like it apart from buckets, console and other sporty features then coming to the fore. Only 1315 were built, though. The completely restyled '63 ($3900) saw only 64 more.

The Park Lane and its convertible returned for '64 (Mercury's silver anniversary year), complementing a $3226 soft-top in that season's baseline Monterey series. Neither was nu-

merous: 1967 and 2592 units, respectively. But volume improved for '65, when the big Mercs were restyled *a la* Lincoln and touted as "fine cars in the Continental tradition." The ragtop Monterey garnered 4762 orders, the Park Lane 6853. For '66, the S-55 returned as a separate series. Its convertible, priced at a reasonable $3614, saw only 669 copies. Demoted to a Monterey sub-series the following year, S-55 scored only 145 convertibles, then was canned.

Meantime, the soft-top 1967 Park Lane was down to 1191 units, the

Monterey to 2673. After equally low numbers of '68s, the full-size Mercs were all-new for '69, when Marquis ousted Park Lane as the top-line series. A convertible continued there, a handsome beast and more Lincoln-like than ever, but volume didn't improve much, totaling 2319. The standard Monterey model was still around, though barely at just 1297 units. Mercury would continue big convertibles through 1971, then gave up.

The Comet, Mercury's compact, received its first convertibles for 1963, paralleling same for that year's Ford

Falcon. Bench-seat Custom and bucket-seat S-22 models, offered at $2557/$2710, racked up over 13,000 sales between them, a big part of Mercury's 1963 ragtop record. After the 1962–63 Meteor failed to make the hoped-for impression in the mid-size field, Comet was elongated and embellished to fill in. A lone convertible was available for 1964–65, in the second-from-top Caliente series, priced around $2650 and good for just over 15,000 units a year.

For 1966, Comet became a true intermediate and offered three convertibles: the Caliente, plus base and GT models in that year's newly expanded high-performance Cyclone series. The latter was Mercury's rival to the likes of the Pontiac GTO, Olds 4-4-2 and Dodge Coronet R/T. Powered by Ford's 335-bhp 390 V-8, the Cyclone offered a variety of useful suspension options. The '67 was even more exciting with its new 427 option. Similar street racers were available among the all-new 1968 models—but not as convertibles, the Cyclones and Caliente being dropped in favor of a single offering in that year's new luxury Montego MX series; it lasted but a single season. None of these mid-size Merc drop-tops sold more than about 2000 units a year except for the '66 Caliente (3922) and '68 Montego (3248). As we'll see, Ford did somewhat better with topless intermediates, helped immeasurably by the showroom drawing power of the Mustang.

Mercury was late in getting a version of the Mustang, but its new-for-'67 Cougar was smashing: longer and more luxurious than the Ford, identified by an "electric shaver" grille and sequential rear turn signals. Convertibles had to wait until 1969, when Cougar became longer and wider, somewhat fussier in appearance, and adopted ventless side glass. Like the original hardtop, the open Cougar came in plain-vanilla and XR7 guise, the latter with rich leather seat trim and comprehensive instrumentation surrounded by simulated walnut. Pro-

Everybody was on the convertible bandwagon in 1965: Cadillac Eldorado, $6738 (*top left*); Chrysler 300, $3911 (*above left*); Chevrolet Impala Super Sport, $3212 (*above center*); Ford Falcon Futura, $2481 (*above*). More '65s (*top right and down*): Dodge Dart GT, $2628; Ford Mustang Official Pace Car for the '65 Indianapolis 500 race; Mustang with GT package, $2614 base; Ford Galaxie 500 XL, $3498. Amazingly, over 100,000 Mustang ragtops were built for the model year.

Still more '65s (*this page, top row*): Lincoln
Continental, $6938; Mercury Monterey, $3230;
Mercury Comet Caliente (*second row*), $2664;
Plymouth Valiant Signet, $2561; Oldsmobile Ninety-
Eight (*opposite page and down*), $4493; Plymouth
Sport Fury, $3209; Pontiac GTO, $3057; and Pontiac
Bonneville, $3594. The Oldsmobile 4-4-2 (*above*),
$3118 when new, is the lone '66 here.

duction came to about 6000 standards and 4000 XR7s. Perhaps reflecting Mercury's diffidence toward convertibles, the hottest '69 Cougar, the new Eliminator, was offered only as a hardtop.

Ford Division may have abandoned the retractable, but it served up a variety of memorable Sixties softtops. Prime among them was the singular 1962–63 Thunderbird Sports Roadster—not a roadster at all but a special version of the normal open Bird.

While convertibles had never accounted for more than about an eighth of T-Bird sales, they were important image-builders. For 1961's third-generation design, Ford began considering how it might answer the constant clamor for a new two-seater. Lee Iacocca, installed as division general manager in 1960, approved the Sports Roadster as an inexpensive way to satisfy that small but vocal demand without tooling up a whole new body.

Designer Bud Kaufman came up with a fiberglass tonneau to cover the normal convertible's back-seat area, giving it faired-in headrests for the front buckets. He also overcame fitting problems so that the top could be raised or lowered with the cover in place. Kelsey-Hayes wire wheels were standard, and the stock rear fender skirts were left off to accommodate them.

The result was striking, but at a hefty $5439—$650 more than the regular T-Bird convertible—the Sports Roadster attracted few buyers: only 1427 for the '62 and just 455 for the near-identical '63. The model was duly canceled for '64, though a similar tonneau became a dealer option for the regular convertible. (Few were sold.) Topless T-Bird demand peaked that year, then declined rapidly. Model year 1966 thus saw the last of the flock, 5049 in all. For 1967, the hardtop was enlarged and an even larger four-door sedan added, beginning the "big Bird" era that would last through 1976.

Mustang was a far more successful idea (one generally, though not accurately, ascribed to Iacocca). It took Detroit by storm with record first-year sales for a new model: 680,000 from its April 1964 introduction through the end of model year '65. Built to a price (about $2500 base) using off-the-shelf components, Mustang succeeded by dint of pretty, long-hood/short-deck

This page, clockwise from top: Dodge fielded five
convertibles for 1966, among them a Coronet 500.
Ford offered the Fairlane 500 XL GT, the last
soft-top Thunderbird, and the popular Mustang.
Chevrolet, meanwhile, did well with the Impala
Super Sport. *Opposite page, from top:* More '66s:
Imperial Crown, Lincoln Continental four-door,
Mercury S-55 (669 built), and the Pontiac GTO.

styling and a myriad of options by which customers could make it anything from economy compact to road-burning grand tourer.

For once, a convertible generated serious volume: 101,945 units in Mustang's first, extra-long model year—15 percent of total production. The top-less Mustang, in fact, was a big reason for the industry's record soft-top sales in '65. Yet this initial flood seemed to satiate demand. By 1967, the convertible was the slowest-selling of Mustang's three body styles, then dropped to fewer than 15,000 units two years later.

A similar fate awaited Ford's other convertibles. The division entered the decade with a handful, had eight by 1966, then slimmed to six by 1970. Four years later there'd be none, though the convertible Mustang would be back.

Falcon was the biggest smash of the Big Three's original 1960 compacts: cleanly styled, cheap, reliable and simple. Like Corvair and Valiant, it soon moved slightly upmarket with the help of folding-top models, but Falcon's wouldn't last long: introduced as a bucket-seat Futura for 1963, then dropped for '66 in deference to the Mustang convertible. There was also a Futura Sprint companion, a mid-1963 addition with standard buckets-and-console interior, tachometer, and Falcon's first V-8 option: the smooth, potent 260-cid small-block, upgraded with more horsepower for '65 as the 289. Unusually modest production makes Sprint convertibles the most collectible Falcons by far: 4602 of the '63s, 4278 of the '64s and just 300 of the '65s.

Ford's full-size Sunliner continued throughout the decade in the top-line series: Galaxie for 1960–61, Galaxie 500 thereafter. Bucket-seat 500XL versions were available from "1962½," renamed plain XL for 1969. The posh LTD, a new Galaxie sub series for '65 and top of the line thereafter, wasn't offered as a ragtop until 1966, and then only for a year, when a lush "7-Litre" sub-model appeared with standard 428 big-block V-8. Just 2368 were built.

Most of these big Fords carried the workhorse 390 V-8. All were burly, luxurious cars on 119-inch wheelbases through 1968, 121 inches for the puffed-up '69. Most were handsome, too, and none were really ugly. Peak

production occurred with the '62 models—55,829 units—which reflects the dwindling interest in sporty big cars that occurred throughout the industry as the decade wore on.

The intermediate Fairlane, new for '62, was another Ford hit, if a somewhat smaller one than Falcon and Mustang. Convertibles weren't available until the enlarged second generation of 1966-67, when Fairlane 500, 500XL and XL GT models appeared, the last with standard 390 V-8 or, less typically, the muscular 427. The midsize Fords were completely redesigned for '68, becoming a bit larger and heavier and gaining curvier "coke-bottle" styling. Ragtops were down to two: a $2822 bench-seat Fairlane 500

and a $3001 bucket-seat GT in the new upper-crust Torino series. Fairlane convertible assemblies usually numbered 4000-6000 a year, though some individual models saw fewer. The '67 500XL, for instance, ran to just 1943 examples, the GT to 2117, the '69 Torino GT to 2552.

General Motors was the company with the most to lose from the convertible's steady sales slide in the late Sixties. Four of its five divisions invariably figured among the top five convertible producers, and the fifth, Cadillac, was never far behind. For 1965, the year Detroit built half a million ragtops, GM contributed over 300,000, and well over a third of those were Chevrolets.

Mustang may have been the Sixties most successful model, but Chevrolet was the decade's most successful make. For 30 years it had been the nation's best-seller; it remained so in the Sixties, not least because of a steadily expanding product line that stretched in every direction—even up into the lower reaches of luxury-car territory. Naturally, this made for a great variety of convertibles.

The two-seat Corvette was always important in this respect, even after the classic Sting Ray coupe arrived for 1963 as an alternative to the customary "roadster." Helped by a $200-$300 price advantage, convertible 'Vettes handily outsold coupes through 1968. Then the coupe took hold, not least be-

140

cause it became a semi-open style—the first "T-top," in fact—offering much of the roadster's open-air feel without its usual drawbacks.

Corvette volume passed 10,000 for the first time with the 1960 models, little changed from the '59s. GM design chief Bill Mitchell gave the '61s a handsome new "ducktail," while the touched-up '62s introduced the 327-cid small-block that would be Corvette's mainstay V-8 through 1965.

Then came the Sting Ray, with exciting Mitchell styling on a four-inch shorter wheelbase (98 inches) and Corvette's first independent rear suspension, engineered by Zora Arkus-Duntov. Sales broke 20,000 units that season, and continued upward each

year except for a modest decline in '67. Styling progressively improved too, and performance got a big boost from big-block V-8s beginning in '65, the last year for fuel injection and the first for disc brakes.

Corvette was rebodied for '68, becoming bigger, brasher and more begadgeted. Motor-noters hooted it for that, as well as decidedly sloppy workmanship, but there were more buyers than ever: close to 40,000 for the '69s. By that point, the open Corvette started at $4438, up from 1960's $3872 base price.

Not quite as sporty, but at least of temporary importance in the soft-top picture, was Chevy's rear-engine Corvair—a failure in its original role as

Top row: Among the hot rods of 1967 was the Buick Skylark GS 400 (*left*). Offered as coupe, hardtop, or convertible, it came with a 401-cid V-8 that pumped out 340 horses. Buick built only 2140 GS 400 soft-tops that year. Chevy gave the '66 a handsome facelift for '67, and still listed the Impala SS soft-top (*right*). It sold for $3149 with the 250-cid six, but a 385-bhp 427 could be ordered. *Bottom row*: The '67 Camaro (*left*) was Chevy's answer to the Mustang. Convertible prices started at $2704 (six cylinder), but two-thirds were V-8 powered and most carried a host of options. The Mustang (*right*) was reskinned for 1967, and a bit bigger. The ragtop sold for $2698 with the 200-cid six, but the 320-bhp 390 was more exciting. Convertible output reached 44,808 units.

economy car, a sensation as a bucket-seat sports compact. Open Corvairs were first offered for '62 in Monza and new turbocharged Monza Spyder form. The pair garnered a healthy 44,000 sales the following year.

Unfortunately, the Corvair's promise and clever approach to efficient motoring was cut short in mid-stride—first by its failure to rival the new Mustang despite 1965's handsome, all-new second-generation design, then by the infamous campaign waged against it by Ralph Nader, who condemned the '65 model for a fault in the 1960 suspension, though the Corvair chassis had been completely fixed by '64. In any case, 1965–69 brought the last open Corvairs: Monza and, through 1966, a new uplevel Corsa model with optional turbo-power. The latter ran to 8353 and 3142 units for 1965–66, respectively. Monza began at around 26,500, plummeted by over half for '66 and sank to 1386 units two years later. Production of the final '69s: a mere 521.

Incidentally, Corvair convertible prices remained remarkably stable. The '62 Monza listed at $2483 base or $2846 in Spyder form; the '69 was less than $200 more. Today, the ragtops are among the rarest of Corvairs, and highly sought-after as both Corvairs and convertibles.

Other Chevy model lines were

Two '67s: Pontiac GTO (*below*) and Corvette (*top right*). Plymouth built 2840 '68 Barracuda soft-tops (*above*). *Opposite page, second row:* Ford's Torino (*left*) paced the '68 Indy 500 while Chevy peddled Impala SS ragtops for $3197. *Bottom row:* "Dodge Fever" afflicted the Coronet 500 (*left*); Pontiac's Bonneville grew a bigger proboscis.

equally replete with convertibles. The full-size Impala series offered a standard bench-seat model throughout the decade, plus a sporty SS variant for 1962–67 (it reverted to option status for 1968–69). A similar arrangement prevailed in the 1962–63 Chevy II line, which arrived as the economy compact Corvair had failed to be. The Chevy II Nova and SS ragtops were dropped when the intermediate Chevelle debuted for 1964 with two convertibles:

Malibu and bucket-seat Malibu SS with choice of six or V-8.

Then came Camaro, taking careful aim at Mustang beginning with model year '67. A convertible was part of its arsenal from the first. A few received the potent Z-28 engine/suspension package that won the Trans-Am Championship for Chevy in 1968–69. A sprightly performer with a wide range of V-8s and other options, the Camaro tallied upwards of a quarter-

million annual sales in its early years and soon overhauled Mustang. But GM design chief Mitchell never thought much of the first-generation design: "No damn good—too many people involved." Convertibles accounted for as small a portion of Camaro sales as they did Mustang's, and when Mitchell got around to creating a Camaro more to his liking, the second-generation design announced for "1970½," it appeared as a coupe only.

This page: Given its yacht-like size, is it any wonder they put wood planking on the '68 Mercury Parklane (*above*). Pontiac built 3518 Tempest Custom convertibles in 1968 (*below*). *Opposite page, from top*: Four 1969 ragtops: Buick Skylark Custom, $3152, 6552 built; Chevrolet Chevelle, with SS 396 package; Chevrolet Camaro, with Rally Sport option; Pontiac Firebird with 400 package.

GM's number-two convertible outfit—and after 1967, number two in the industry—was Pontiac, riding high on the sporty image established when Bunkie Knudsen became division general manager back in '57. Pontiac's commitment to the convertible market was enormous: full-size Catalina and Bonneville; compact and mid-size Tempest, Tempest Le Mans and GTO; the Catalina-based 1966 2+2 and '67 Grand Prix (the latter a one-year-only version of Pontiac's big personal-luxury car with just 5876 built); and the Camaro-clone 1967–69 Firebird.

The legendary GTO was undoubtedly Pontiac's greatest Sixties convertible. Introduced in mid-1964—and, unlike many others of its ilk, offered as a convertible from day one—it started the muscle-car phenomenon that would soon sweep the industry and buyers off their feet. No wonder: With the proper options, a GTO could trim any other six-passenger car on the road.

To order a '64 GTO convertible, you began with a $2641 Tempest Custom or $2796 Tempest Le Mans drop-top, then plunked down an extra $300 for the GTO package, which included 389 V-8, quick steering, stiff shocks, dual exhausts and premium tires. Four-speed manual gearbox cost $188, sintered metallic brake linings, H.D. radiator and limited-slip differential added $75. Another $115 bought a 360-bhp 389; by that point, all you needed was a lead foot and lots of gas.

The GTO convertible continued past the end of the decade and always sold well for such a specialized car: up to 10,000 a year. In retrospect, it's the most desirable Pontiac convertible of the Sixties. Maybe ever.

Oldsmobile and Buick, while not at Pontiac's volume, continued to produce lots of topless cars throughout the Sixties. Oldsmobile consistently offered one in each of its model lines, from compact F-85/Cutlass to full-size 98. There was also a special Super/Delta 88 ragtop in 1961–66, the buckets-and-console Starfire. Its annual volume ranged from 2236 (1965) to 13,019 (1966), with 4000 or 7000 in most years.

Olds' answer to GTO was the 4-4-2, introduced as an option package at mid-'64, then made a separate model from 1966. A convertible was available each year. The designation originally

denoted four-speed gearbox, four-barrel carb and dual exhausts; a 400 V-8 replaced the initial 330 for '65 and was factored into the model name. The 4-4-2 package cost only about $250 that year, a bargain. Included were special road wheels; heavy-duty springs and shocks; beefed-up rear axle, driveshaft and engine mounts; special frame and steering ratio; stabilizer bars front and rear; fat tires; 11-inch-diameter clutch; 70-amp battery and special trim. Performance was on the order of 7.5 seconds 0-60 mph, the quarter-mile in 17 seconds at 85 mph.

Each successive 4-4-2 was eagerly awaited. The 400 V-8 was never pushed much beyond 350 bhp, but it

was enough. Especially in convertible guise, the 4-4-2 was good-looking and capable, a road car that handled and stopped as well as it accelerated and cruised. The '69s had big i.d. numerals, black-finish grille and a set of hood bulges—a bit juvenile, but distinctive.

Occupying a somewhat more adult market sector with rather higher-priced cars, Buick built less extroverted convertibles than Olds and Pontiac, but lots of them. Like Oldsmobile, Buick had one in most every model line, from the compact and intermediate Special/Skylark through the big LeSabre, Invicta/Wildcat and long-wheelbase Electra 225.

The Gran Sport and Wildcat were

Buick's most memorable Sixties softtops. The latter began in 1962 as a special Invicta hardtop. A convertible and hardtop sedan were added the next year; Wildcat then replaced Invicta for '64. Most Wildcats had bucket seats, and all were offered with brawny V-8s that ran to a 325-bhp 401. The GS, a sporty Special/Skylark evolution, also began as a trim package, for '66.

Buick's biggest engine ever arrived for 1967: a new 430 V-8, standard on Wildcat, Electra and the svelte Riviera personal-luxury coupe. It had little more horsepower than the 401, but was quieter and smoother-running. Also new was a 400 for intermediates,

146

Five '69 ragtops (clockwise from left): Plymouth Barracuda with 'Cuda 340 option, which added $309.35 to the $3082 base price; Mercury Cougar XR7, $3595, the first Cougar convertible, 4024 built; Pontiac Firebird 400, 11,649 soft-tops built; Road Runner, $3313, Plymouth's first "beep, beep" convertible, 2128 built; Chevrolet Corvette, $4438, 16,608 ragtops produced.

appearing on a GS400 convertible and hardtop coupe; the open version started at near $3200.

Cadillac finished fifth or sixth in convertibles each year, underlining its traditional high appeal to moneyed luxury-minded buyers. This didn't require much model diversity either. Through 1966, Cadillac got by with one Series 62/DeVille convertible at around $6000 and an upmarket Eldorado Biarritz some $1000 higher. The latter vanished for '67, when Eldorado was reborn as a front-drive coupe, but the soft-top DeVille continued to account for about 17,000 sales each model year. This made Cadillac a major convertible producer, its volume ex-

ceeded only by that of ostensibly more popular makes like Plymouth, Dodge and Mercury.

The outlandish tailfinned '59s soon gave way to more conservative Cadillacs as Bill Mitchell designs began replacing those of his predecessor as GM styling chief, Harley Earl (who'd retired in '58). The '61s were cleaner than any Cadillacs in years. The make's long-running V-8 was revised for 1963 with a stiffer block, lighter and stronger crankshaft and new accessory mounting points. All were notable steps toward the ultimate in smooth, quiet power, always a Cadillac objective. The major changes for 1965 were a lower silhouette and the end of

tailfins. In 1966, Cadillac Division recorded its first 200,000-car year.

Studebaker excepted, the Sixties ended with the same automakers as had started the decade. For the convertible, however, it was a topsy-turvy 10 years. In 1969, just four years after scoring record production, convertibles barely made it over the 200,000 mark, and changes in model lineups and body production for 1970 suggested that their ranks would be thinner still in years to come.

In short, America's 1965 sweetheart had been spurned almost overnight. The reasons are not difficult to fathom. You'll find them in the next chapter.

The redesigned 1970 Plymouth Barracuda saw only
635 'Cuda convertibles built, here with the
standard 335-bhp 383 V-8. Price: $3433.

When Cadillac Motor Car Division announced that its 1976 Eldorado, by then America's sole production convertible, would be the last of its kind, humanity's baser instincts were revealed in a period of national silliness. "Buff books," which had long ignored it, rushed to publish tearful obituaries, while the general media blamed the convertible's demise on everything from Detroit bean-counters to malaise in the national spirit.

Newsweek's postmortem was typical: "To a couple of generations, the sleek, sassy convertible conjured up an image of the hep young playboy and his stunning girlfriend—her hair always flying in the wind...And now that the U.S. has developed freeways that invite intoxicating speed, air that chokes with carbon monoxide and a growing concern for safety that does not mesh with roofless automobiles, the once-coveted convertible appears headed for the great junkyard of nostalgia."

The facts are that the national speed limit had, since 1974, been a laughable figure nobody respected; that except possibly for the Los Angeles basin, the nation's air had been getting cleaner, not dirtier, since 1968; that the number of people killed in convertible rollovers who would have survived under steel tops was infinitesimal. Evidently, the magazine—and some of its readers no doubt—ignored or were unaware of these.

Then there were the self-flagellators, a common breed since Viet Nam, who opined that the fault lay with—you guessed it—us. "If the car buyers of America let the convertible die," wrote one Gary Seever of Minneapolis, "then all these people deserve is a four-door sedan shaped like a box, painted flat black, and equipped with a six and stick." Well, there would be a time in the Seventies when the public *did* seem to prefer such cars.

Perhaps the greatest ignorance was exhibited by those expected to have the most smarts: the buff publications. According to *Motor Trend*, the convertible died because "1) The government has begun proposing roof-strength specifications; 2) neither the hardtop nor convertible provides suitable low-angle mounting points for mandatory shoulder harness; 3) GM stylists felt it was time for some basic changes in

Buick's least expensive full size convertible in 1970 was the LeSabre Custom (*above*). It rode a 124-inch wheelbase and came with a 260-bhp version of the 350 V-8. Prices started at $3700 and 2487 were built. Cadillac's only soft top that year was the de Ville (*left*). It measured 129.5 inches between the wheels and the 472-cid V-8 cranked out 375 horsepower. Even at $6068, sales were brisk; 15,172 were built.

This page: Ford built 6348 full-size XL
convertibles in 1970 (*top*), while Oldsmobile
turned out 2933 mid-size 4-4-2s (*above*).
Opposite, from top: The '70 'Cuda looks mean
coming or going. The Challenger shared its body
and drivetrain with the Barracuda. Dodge sold
1070 high-performance R/T ragtops that year.

body design and concluded that the pillared sedan was the way to go in view of the market picture."

But *Motor Trend* and the others were wrong too. Federal rollover standards were never enacted, the shoulder-harness mount proved no problem (as today's reborn convertibles demonstrate) and GM product planners decreed a switch to pillared bodies mainly for economic reasons.

There was also this explanation: "Now the car is a paragon of luxury, silence, ease and security," wrote *MT*'s Fred Gregory. "People don't go motoring anymore. They cruise, shut off the world behind tinted glass in a padded cubicle, having no communion with the road, the car or the outside atmosphere. But for the minimal demands of power-assisted steering, they may as well be in a pressurized 747."

How, then, did brother Gregory explain that, as domestic convertibles vanished, British Leyland—hardly ever successful at anything, but a major supplier of soft-top cars by 1975—suddenly tallied record U.S. sales? Or, more important, how the public's buying habits flip-flopped 40 percent between 1973 and '75—from "pressurized 747s" to cars that "communed with the road"?

Of all the car monthlies, *Motor Trend* should have known better. But hindsight is cheap, and editor Mike Knepper deserves credit for naming the *real* trouble: declining sales. "I have owned convertibles," he wrote, "but I don't own one now. I am part of the reason the convertible is passing... We quit buying them, so Detroit quit building them... Yes, it's the end of an era. I loved it. And I'll miss it." (Like a four-foot-long poodle?) "It's unfortunate some die-hard romantic in Detroit couldn't have seen fit to keep at least one convertible in production after this year." Well...gee. Romantics are seldom captains of industry.

Of course, the big joke on all the doomsayers was that, as Mark Twain would have said, reports of the convertible's death were greatly exaggerated. Technically, you see, the ragtop never really died in the U.S.—not with topless imports from VWs to Rolls-Royces, convertible conversions of domestic coupes (which began appearing even before that last '76 Eldo) and the Jeep CJ. And guess what? A new generation of American convertibles would be born in 1982, beginning with Lee Iacocca and Chrysler Corporation. Of course, Iacocca revived the body style for money, not love, his autobiography notwithstanding.

Still, the fact remains that American "factory" convertibles were absent nearly six years because they hadn't sold. But why hadn't they? Moreover, how could their sales plunge so drastically within five years of setting an all-time record?

Pat Chappell, writing in *The Milestone Car* in 1976, said one reason was that buyers had a convertible alternative as early as 1955: the two-door hardtop, which jumped ahead of the two-door sedan for the first time that year to assume a dominant role in Detroit production. She then quoted a leading consumer magazine: "While retaining the winter comfort of a closed car, the hardtop embodies the sporty look of the convertible...The 'ragtop' offers less protection than a hardtop in a rollover accident. A convertible is expensive to buy, and added maintenance costs are likely to be high as well. The undeniable pleasure of top-down driving on ideal days may well be offset, in cold climates, by the undeniable difficulty of keeping the car warm in winter." One wonders if they ever tried the heater in a Chrysler Windsor.

In 1972, that same magazine condemned the hardtop: "The 4-door sedan...is less given to rattles, squeaks, and drafts, it offers more protection in a roll-over accident and it's easier to get into and out of the rear seat." A year later, the magazine was pleased to report that "fewer pillarless hardtops are being sold," but was starting to worry about "a number of sedans with thin pillars." Apparently, the editors didn't think body construction had advanced a jot since 1955.

A second factor came into play around 1955: imports. Before the Volkswagen, whose sales first alarmed Detroit that year, foreign cars had been small potatoes in the vast U.S. market. But many had been convertibles or roadsters—Jaguars, MGs, Triumphs—and experience with all kinds of imports began increasing buyer dissatisfaction with Detroit cars. The ranks of these customers swelled dramatically in the Sixties and reached Herculean proportions by the mid-Seventies, which spelled big trouble for Detroit's market share in general and the convertible's in particular. In fact, the American convertible was ex-

actly the type of car these people would have bought had they not been hooked on imports.

Take your typical 1970 "yuppie" (known back then as "fast-rising college grad") earning $12,000 a year, weaned on Oldsmobiles and driving a soft-top '66 Ninety-Eight. Converted to imports by a friend's dead-reliable Bug or a neighbor's flashy Jaguar, he or she shops for a new convertible. But is it a $7000 Cadillac DeVille? No, it's a $2500 ragtop Beetle, a $3500 MGB or, disposable income permitting, a $7000 Mercedes 280SL. Bang! One Detroit customer lost, repeated many times.

We should also not forget the trage-

dy of Viet Nam, which claimed 58,000 young people and maimed thousands more. It's likely that many would have bought convertibles, especially the muscle-car variety. And we all know that muscle cars withered as much as convertibles in 1965–75.

A final nail in the convertible's coffin was the simple march of technology: the advent and almost universal adoption of more efficient and affordable air conditioning systems; sealing, sound-isolation and other body improvements that really *did* render closed cars far quieter and more comfortable than convertibles; and the arrival of sunroofs and moonroofs,

which provided seven-tenths of a convertible's feel with none of the inconvenience.

But enough sociology and on to the cars. Statistics tell much of the story:

Year	Convertibles	% of Market
1965	509,419	5.48
1969	201,997	2.46
1970	91,863	1.40
1974	27,955	0.50

American Motors had abandoned convertibles after 1968. Chrysler Corporation followed suit after 1971, going from 11 to three in just one year.

Considering its future role in reviving them, the Chrysler marque's early abandoning of convertibles is ironic. The 1970 Newport and 300, on the 124-inch wheelbase used for all models that year except Town & Country wagons, would be the last Chrysler convertibles until 1982. A number of die-hards flocked to buy them, though too few. Only 1124 Newports and 1077 300s were built, all early in the model year.

As an artifact, the 300 is to be preferred today. It came with the big 440-cubic-inch V-8, offering 350/375 gross horsepower. Newports had a 383, with the 440 optional. The 300's base price was $4580 against $3925 for the Newport, but a low-mileage original 300 is now worth 50 percent more than a comparable Newport—and both bring more than what they cost new, albeit in inflated dollars.

Dodge and Plymouth opened the decade with more elaborate convertible programs that dissolved in a hurry. Dodge's 1970 line included five ragtops in three model groups. The new 110-inch-wheelbase Challenger ponycar and mid-size 117-inch Coronet 500 contained base and sportier R/T models (the latter offering a 440 option). The 122-inch-wheelbase Polara V-8, that year's base full-size Dodge, carried a $3500 convertible.

The R/Ts were probably over-engined, especially the Challenger, though they did have carefully tuned (if hard-riding) chassis to handle the big-block's power. And they remained the clean, speedy-looking Detroit-style grand tourers R/Ts had been in the Sixties. But the market just wasn't there. Dodge duly yanked all but the base Challenger convertible for '71. Collectors should note Dodge's modest early-Seventies ragtop volume:

Dodge Convertible Production 1970–71

Year/Model	Total
1970 Challenger	3,173
1970 Challenger R/T	1,070
1970 Coronet 500	924
1970 Coronet R/T	296
1970 Polara Deluxe	842
1971 Challenger	2,165

Plymouth's convertibles paralleled Dodge's except for an additional version of the hulkier, heavier new 1970 Barracuda. The Challenger, of course, was Dodge's belated ponycar, planned alongside the third-generation Barracuda but aimed more at Mercury Cougar than Ford Mustang. Both arrived for 1970 sharing basic underbody structure, chassis and drivetrains, though the Dodge rode a two-inch longer wheelbase and differed in some styling elements. Both tailed off to just two closed models for 1973–74, then vanished.

Like Challenger, the third-generation Barracuda took a "more ponycar" approach to a market that was still strong at the time development work commenced. The new design feature

Full-size convertibles from General Motors: (*opposite, from top*): The 1970 Chevrolet Impala listed at $3377, found 9562 buyers. The '71 Cadillac Eldorado cost a whopping $7751; output reached 6800. *This page*: Pontiac built 3037 Bonnevilles at $4040 apiece (*top*), while Buick produced only 2161 Centurions at $4678.

The '71 Dodge Challenger R/T was chosen as the Official Pace Car for the Indianapolis 500, which was run on May 29, 1971. Accordingly, 50 "Hemi-Orange" convertibles, all with white interiors, were prepared for use during pre-race festivities. Two were equipped with heavy-duty equipment: the actual Pace Car and a back-up car.

for both was provision for big-block engines, up to and including the jumbo 440 and fiery 425-horsepower street hemi. So equipped, the ragtops bid fair as the fastest of Detroit's 1970–71 herd.

Partly because they were new, these Clydesdales enjoyed good 1970 sales. But ponycar demand was shrinking fast and GM's new Camaro/Firebird was strong competition, so both suffered mightily thereafter. Challenger sales dropped by 60 percent in one year, from 83,000 for 1970 to some 30,000 of the '71s. Barracuda fared worse, falling from about 58,000 to 18,690. In both cases, most of those sold were hardtop coupes.

The 1970 Barracudas comprised hardtop and convertible in standard, luxury Gran Coupe and performance-oriented 'Cuda trim—meaning that, yes, you could buy a "Gran Coupe convertible," though only in 1970. Ragtop prices that year ran $3034 to $3433. The standard cars came with a six; Gran Coupes carried the venerable 318 V-8 as standard, the muscle-laden 'Cudas a 383.

Like Dodge, Plymouth reprised standard and sporty intermediate convertibles and one full-size model for 1970. Respectively, these were Satellite, Road Runner and Fury III. The mid-size GTX and big Sport Fury models did not return from '69. The Satellite name had replaced Belvedere on Plymouth intermediates for '68, the year Road Runner was introduced. The '70 line marked the last of this mid-size generation—and mid-size Plymouth ragtops.

All of which makes the 1970 RR convertible a highly desirable collector's item today. Named for the beloved Warner Brothers cartoon character, the Runner still came with cartoon decals and "beep-beep" horn. As before, the '70 lived up to that name: Tightly sprung, it cornered as if on rails and went like almighty clappers when it had to (which was most of the time for many owners). V-8s were the same stalwart array 'Cudas offered, including the street hemi.

But 1971's swoopy new-generation design gave Chrysler a convenient excuse for forgetting mid-size Dodge and Plymouth convertibles, hence their termination. As a hardtop, the Road Runner would survive through 1975. Then Chrysler abandoned performance cars across the board and the

Runner became a "paint-on performance" version of the compact Volaré—about which the less said the better.

The Fury III was Plymouth's best-selling soft-top in these years, the top of the full-size line ($3415 for 1970) save the hardtop Sport Fury GT and exotic Superbird. But it was all relative: Plymouth convertible volume shrunk just like Dodge's:

Plymouth Convertible Production 1970–71

Year/Model	Total
1970 Barracuda	1,554
1970 Barracuda Gran Coupe	596
1970 'Cuda	636
1970 Satellite	701
1970 Road Runner	824
1970 Fury III	1,952
1971 Barracuda	1,014
1971 'Cuda	374

For Ford Motor Company, it was, as the philosopher said, a case of "the same story, only more so." The convertible took longer to die at Dearborn, but the handwriting was on the wall. Lincoln had given up after 1967; Mercury averaged about 4000 a year in 1970–73, Ford about 13,000. By that point, the only ones left were Mustang and Cougar. Both were scrubbed for '74, when Cougar became a fat-cat intermediate and the original ponycar was replaced by the underwhelming Mustang II.

The end of the drop-top Mustang seemed inconceivable, for the convertible had been a big part of Mustang's early success. Though it found fewer buyers as the years passed, it was always there, touted with let-them-eat-cake praise and prominent in the brochures. Maybe it doesn't sell, Ford seemed to be saying, but it sure helps Mustang's image.

And Ford product planners gave the convertible their best possible shot. Unlike Chrysler and GM rivals, the topless Mustang was never diluted by sub-models. There was always just one, albeit with the usual long list of options, including wild engines. And it did have a following, a much larger one than other roofless ponycars. When Ford announced that the 1973 Mustang ragtop would be the last, dealers moved close to 12,000, 50 percent more than the annual total for 1970–72.

Ford's other convertibles were a prosaic lot, few in number, and sooner extinct. The intermediate Torino, restyled for 1970 into one of Dearborn's ugliest cars ever, offered its last soft-top for '71, a GT model (1613 sold). The full-size Ford did better, recording 6348 XL sales for 1970 and 5750/4234 for 1971–72, when it finally shifted to the top-line LTD series. Unabashedly big and luxurious, the LTD started at $4500 and was typically optioned to well over $5000.

Predictably, Mercury still mostly followed Ford's convertible strategy. An exception was the continuation of standard and XR-7 Cougars for 1970–73. Priced about $500 above the soft-top Mustang, they still aimed at better-heeled types. Trouble was, few such buyers seemed to want convertibles now. Though much larger and heavier than the original, these Cougars were nice-looking, well-appointed cars—and quick when equipped with one of the 351 or 428 V-8s—but 4000 units a year was hardly impressive volume for an outfit like Lincoln-Mercury.

Unlike Ford, Mercury gave up on mid-size drop-tops after 1969. Its only other offerings were gigantic, 124-inch-wheelbase Monterey and Marquis models that respectively garnered 581 and 1233 sales for 1970, their final year.

The sheer size and product spread of General Motors virtually assured that the world's largest automaker would field the most convertibles of the Big Three and stay with them the longest. But even GM couldn't escape the market's turn from topless motoring. Its offerings thus dwindled from 18 different 1970 models to six by '73. Three years later, the Cadillac Eldorado would be the only drop-top Detroiter left.

The Chevrolet Corvette convertible persisted through 1975, though the companion T-top coupe had surpassed it in sales in 1969 and took an increasing share of each subsequent year's pie. The final edition saw only 4629 copies, the lowest production for an open Corvette since 1956. Interestingly, Corvette performance took a dive at the same time. For 1970, a new 454-cid enlargement of Chevy's big-block V-8, designed to better meet emissions standards, replaced the previously optional 427s. But the most powerful (465-bhp) version planned was never offered because it couldn't be cleaned up enough

to satisfy the "revenooers." For the same reason, the solid-lifter 350 LT-1 small-block option bit the dust after 1970.

Such changes took big bites out of Corvette's top power ratings: 460 bhp for 1970, 425 for '71, 270 for '72 (SAE net), 205 by 1975. This plus new federally mandated safety equipment made a change in the car's character inevitable. By 1975, Corvette had become a more balanced car—less outlandish, arguably more pleasant to drive—a plush high-speed GT instead of a stark straight-line screamer.

Yet sales continued strong despite this and the lack of a ragtop. Why? Despite its softer nature, the Vette was one of the few cars still available after mid-decade with anything like traditional Detroit performance. In short, "America's only true sports car" was now one of America's few really exciting cars.

There were two others: the Chevy Camaro Z-28 and Pontiac's Firebird Trans Am. But both these ponycars were out of the ragtop field by virtue of Bill Mitchell's coupe-only second generation of 1970.

Although the muscle car market was fading rapidly, Pontiac still fielded a GTO in 1971, and in no less than four models. Only 661 buyers chose the convertible (top), which sold for $3676. The top-down GTO Judge, at $4070, was truly rare: 17 produced. Oldsmobile did a bit better with the 4-4-2 ragtop (far left)—1304 units were built. It listed at $3743. At the luxury end of the market, the '72 Cadillac Fleetwood Eldorado soft top (left) weighed in ready for the road at two and a half tons and cost a lofty $7546, but 7975 buyers lined up to buy one anyway. It was powered by a huge 500-cubic-inch V-8, but the horsepower rating was only 235 because of the new *net* rating system.

Little topless material appeared in Chevy's other model lines. Through 1972 it consisted of a mid-size Chevelle Malibu and full-size Impala, base-priced at about $3200 and $4000, respectively, but selling for more like $4000/$5000 with popular options. The hot Malibu Super Sport was now an option package, but could be ordered with either the 454, pumping out 425 gross bhp for '71, or a 402-cid, 300-bhp V-8 evolved from the original 396 (and still called that).

GM switched all intermediates to new "Colonnade" styling for 1973, which meant pillared instead of pillarless hardtop coupes and sedans—and no more convertibles. Not counting the Corvette, this left Chevy with just the big convertible, built on the corporate B-body platform with a grand 121.5-inch wheelbase. Reasoning that it might as well shoot for the maximum buck, the division duly spruced up the Impala convertible into a Caprice Classic for 1973. It lasted only three model years.

Though it cost a lot—$4400-$4800 base, some $500-$800 up on the previous Impala—this Caprice was a nice car: roomy, luxurious, a smooth cruiser—and a dinosaur rapidly heading for the automotive tar pits. (In the wake of the 1973–74 fuel crisis, GM had decided to downsize its big cars, the first of which would appear, *sans* convertibles, for 1977.) But people liked it about as much as any convertible in those days, especially once they heard it was going away. The last-of-the-line '75 sold 8339 copies, the highest figure for any Seventies Chevrolet convertible.

As an artifact of how Americans once built cars, the Caprice Classic is about as good an example as you can find. Also worth noting: Clean originals now command well in excess of their sticker prices, suggesting that all of GM's last big convertibles, not just the '76 Eldo, are inexorably becoming collectible automobiles.

Through 1974, Chevrolet continued to lead the industry in convertible volume, stunted though that had become. But with the end of intermediate and ponycar soft-tops, "USA-1" was overhauled in 1975 by Oldsmobile, which had been running it a close second. In fact, Olds built nearly half of all De-

troit's 1975 ragtops and almost twice as many as Chevrolet. You could say that Lansing was among the final holdouts during the convertible's "last days in the bunker."

There was a reason for this, though only one: Olds had made a conscious effort to mop up most of whatever convertible market remained by mid-decade. By that point it had just one mop: a topless Delta 88 Royale, $5200

of full-size, 124-inch-wheelbase luxury cruiser that did what Lansing expected of it.

Contrary to some books, the convertible wasn't the most expensive Delta (some station wagons cost more), but it was certainly impressive. Tipping the scales at a portly 4300 pounds, it offered a healthy helping of standard features: power steering and front disc brakes, deluxe steering

wheel, steel-belted radial tires, and a 170-bhp (SAE net) 350 V-8. Styling after '72 suffered mainly from the 5-mph bumpers found on most big Detroit cars at the time—which gave it the prow of an 18-wheeler.

The Delta Royale was Olds' only convertible after 1972, but sales had been miserable until '75. All the publicity surrounding it (more, in fact, than attended the Caprice) allowed the last

Chevrolet fielded two convertibles in 1972 One was the mid-size Chevelle Malibu, the other the full-size Impala seen here. It rode a 122-inch wheelbase and weighed 4125 pounds. At $3979, it came with a 350 V-8, but a 402 or 454 could be ordered. A total of 6456 units were built.

By 1973, it looked like the end for the Mustang convertible (*top*), and indeed it would be for a decade. However, 11,853 were built, with prices starting at $3102. The '73 Cadillac Eldorado (*above left*) sported the mandated five-mile-per-hour front bumper; 9315 were built. Oldsmobile continued the Delta 88 Royale soft top into 1974 (*above right*), building 3716 that year.

topless Olds to go out a modest success.

Royale aside, few other Olds ragtops survived past 1970. That year saw the last big Ninety-Eight. The next saw the end of the once-popular 4-4-2 muscle car, which reverted to option status for 1972. Like all others, 4-4-2 convertible numbers were low: 2933 of the '70s, 1304 of the '71s. The soft-top mid-size Cutlass, offered from 1970 only as a bucks-up Supreme model, said *adieu* after '72, though it managed a respectable 11,000-plus sales that year. Overall, Oldsmobile gave a dying breed one of its best shots, building well over 80,000 convertibles in 1970–75, second only to Chevrolet.

Buick and Pontiac turned in almost identical performances in the Seventies. Each division built about 15,000 convertibles for 1970, the last significant production year, about 8000 for 1971 and '72 and about half that number for 1973–75.

Five convertibles returned in the 1970 Buick line: the traditional LeSabre/Wildcat/Electra trio, still on enormous 124- and 127-inch wheelbases, and the intermediate Skylark Custom and Gran Sport, the latter mounting a standard 455-cid V-8 with 350/360 bhp. Wildcat (1244 built) and GS 455 (1416) were the rarest, which naturally makes them the most collectible today.

The 455 was a kind of valedictory to the age of big-inch engines. Buick's largest ever, it had a compression ratio of at least 10:1 and returned only 10-12 miles per gallon of premium gas. The most powerful version was also used in 1970's senior Electra 225 series, which included the last Electra convertible.

Minus that one, Buick's ragtops repeated for '71, except that the Wildcat series was renamed Centurion. Convertible sales were broadly lower, the Gran Sport sinking to 902 units, for example. With 1973's "Colonnade" intermediates and cancellation of the ragtop LeSabre, the Centurion was Buick's sole convertible. Then that series was dropped and the convertible became a LeSabre again, offered only in upmarket Custom trim. It, too, would depart after 1975, when production totaled 5300.

Like their divisional counterparts, the big '71 Buicks were as large as American cars would ever get. More rounded styling marked that year's new B/C-body design, with "fuselage" sides, massive hoods and broad ex-

panses of glass. GM's full-sizers continued in this form through 1976, with mainly minor annual changes to meet safety and emissions requirements. Then all were downsized, the first phase of a corporate-wide "big shrink" that would cost a lot more than dollars.

Part of that cost involved a growing uniformity among GM's cars, reflected in its "last" convertibles of the Seventies. Strict market separation, the guiding principle of Al Sloan, had been sacrificed during the expansive Sixties in favor of platforms (in the necessary sizes) shared by as many divisions as possible. To some extent, this was prompted by demands from each dealer group for as many different kinds of cars as possible. But when the market contracted in the early Seventies, GM found itself with too many lookalike, overlapping model lines spread among five makes whose identities were no longer so clear to customers. The similarities began to hurt.

Nowhere was this more apparent than at Pontiac, which mainly marketed the same cars as Buick, Olds and Chevrolet. (Only the names were changed to protect division executives.) Its convertibles thus followed the same pattern. For the record, Pontiac sold full-size soft-tops as a Catalina (1970–72), Bonneville (1970) and Grand Ville (1971–75). Typical yearly production was around 3000-4500 units except 1971–72, when the Catalina and Grand Ville saw fewer than 2500 each.

Also like sister divisions, Pontiac lost its mid-size convertibles with the 1973 "Colonnade" generation. It was just as well, as Pontiac could sell no more than 6000 of any one model in 1970-72. This made for some rather rare ragtops. For instance, the flashy high-performance GTO Judge saw exactly 17 copies for '71, that year's normal GTO 661.

Under division chief John Z. DeLorean, who claimed never to have made a mistake, Pontiac policy had been to outflank Chevy in the low-price field while challenging Olds/Buick in the medium-price ranks. But the results were an untimely blurring of Pontiac's "with it" image, a slide in assembly quality, a pile-up of unsold cars and sales losses to Oldsmobile and Buick. In fact, Olds nosed out Pontiac in 1973 model year registrations, the first time that had happened since 1958; by 1975, both Olds and Buick

were threatening Pontiac's number-three spot. And while Pontiac had usually run fifth in convertible volume, Cadillac surpassed it in 1973.

Cadillac wasn't much affected by such intramural battles. Above the fray in its traditional luxury sector, it continued with a quarter-million or more annual sales in the early Seventies—and to make money with just one convertible. The 1970 model was still a 130-inch-wheelbase DeVille, priced at $6068 that year. Then, with 1971's new C-body, the DeVille was replaced by a soft-top version of the front-drive Eldorado, itself redesigned and grossly enlarged that year. At $7751, the revived Eldo convertible (the first since '66) was more profitable on fewer sales. A good thing, as yearly production hovered around 7500, versus 30,000-40,000 coupes. Nevertheless, as convertibles from other makes vanished, the Eldo came to be a prestige item for Cadillac; one even paced the 1973 Indianapolis 500.

But the deck was stacked against it almost from the first. For 1972, the Eldo hardtop appeared with a new "Custom Cabriolet" option, which meant an electric-sliding steel sunroof over the front seats and an elk-grain-vinyl rear half-roof (complete with "halo" trim molding). The more convenient sunroof, of course, was one of the key developments that hastened the drop-top's demise.

A feature dating back to the original 1953 Eldorado appeared on the '72 convertible: a metal boot or tonneau over the top well. Electronic fuel injection was optional by 1975, when Cadillac proffered another anti-convertible idea: the Astro Roof, a tinted-glass power moonroof with sliding interior sunshade.

The funeral notices for the American convertible mentioned at the beginning of this chapter were prompted by Cadillac's announcement that the '76 Eldorado convertible would be the last. The division even announced production in advance: 14,000—up nearly 60 percent on the '75 total. While that represented the number of convertible tops and mechanisms left in stock, Cadillac was clearly milking this "milestone" for all its worth.

Gripped by last-chance acquisitiveness, buyers beat down the doors—and, figuratively, each other sometimes. "We expect to sell every one," said then general manager Edward C.

Kennard. "I've already received letters from people saying they want to buy the last one. Maybe we should make the last 2000 the same, call it the 'Finale' and get another $200 or $300 for it." (And they wonder why we have consumer advocates.)

Ultimately, the decision was to single out the last *200*. All were painted white and had white tops, wheel covers and upholstery, plus a special dash plaque attesting to "the end of an era."

The '76 Eldorado convertibles, the last 200 in particular, thus became the subjects of a con job more remarkable than the Great South Seas Bubble. Would-be owners began offering well over sticker, which was about $12,000, thus sending delivered prices toward the moon. Dealers, meantime, had naturally stocked up against the expected onslaught of these suckers. Ig-

norant "money" magazines, the more ignorant general media and even the National Automobile Dealers Association *Used Car Guide* touted '76 values well above those for the '75s—as much as *eight years* after they were built.

Unheard in this near hysteria were the voices of experienced car collectors and organizations like the Cadillac-LaSalle Club and Milestone Car Society. The '76 Eldorado convertible, they warned, was about 50 percent more common than the '75; ready-made collector's items are rarely good investments; and new convertibles were still being built if you counted AMC's Jeeps or the imports.

But buyers didn't listen, of course, some paying up to $30,000 for one of these "last convertibles"—proving once again that P.T. Barnum was right about the birth rate of the easily duped. Today, a '76 Eldo convertible is

worth little, if any, more than a '75 in comparable condition. Incidentally, the highest price we could find in a collector-car price guide at this writing is— wait for it—$12,000, the original purchase price (albeit in 1988's less valuable currency).

In 1984, the most ridiculous lawsuit since the Scopes monkey trial cropped up when a couple of lawyers filed a class-action suit against Cadillac on behalf of all who'd bought '76s as investments. Reason? The division had "promised" that the '76 Eldorado would be its last convertible, and here Cadillac was offering them again. Little has been heard of the suit since, which is about what it deserves.

Of course, Cadillac wasn't alone with a revived convertible in 1984. But that story, and the tale of the ragtop's rebirth throughout Detroit, deserves a separate chapter.

By 1975, the Cadillac Fleetwood Eldorado ragtop (*bottom*) had crossed the $10,000 mark. Still, 8950 were built. The '74 Corvette Stingray soft top, listing at $5846, saw production of 5474 units, one-sixth that of the coupe.

New Beginnings

Within six years of being consigned to history, the great American convertible made a somewhat surprising return. You might think it could only happen in Detroit, but that's rather cynical. Besides, this hasn't been the only resurrection of an old favorite. A well-known and more recent example is "Classic" Coke. Sometimes, like the song says, you don't know what you've got til it's gone.

Long ago, Joseph W. Frazer told this writer, "You've gotta have a sense of humor in this business—humor, and a helluva lot of money." People said Lee Iacocca, the extroverted chairman of Chrysler Corporation—formerly the extroverted president of Ford Motor Company—exhibited his sense of humor in reviving the convertible for 1982. He certainly had the money.

The story of how Iacocca, ungratefully canned by Henry Ford II, rode off to save the industry's sick man has almost become part of American folklore—mainly because Iacocca put it there, in his own best-selling autobiography. Of course, history will treat Iacocca kindly because, to paraphrase Sir Winston Churchill, he wrote so much of it himself.

Not so long ago, when things were grim and Chrysler's fate rested largely in the halls of Congress, we writers could ask questions and get direct answers from the boss himself. No more. When I wrote Iacocca to ask him why he decided to start producing convertibles again—and with no marketing studies to justify it—back came a conventional letter from Public Relations. Mr. Iacocca had covered this in his book, they said, and here was a copy (paperback): "See pages 295-296." Okay....

"In 1982, as we began to get healthy again, I decided to bring back the convertible," Iacocca wrote. "As an experiment, I had one built by hand from a Chrysler LeBaron. I drove it over the summer, and I felt like the Pied Piper. People in Mercedes and Cadillacs started running me off the road and pulling me over like a cop. 'What are you driving?' they all wanted to know. 'Who built it? Where can I get one?'

"When they recognized my now

The Mustang GT was restyled for 1987 with spoilers, spats, and a more aerodynamic nose. As an '88, it boasts 225 bhp and a $16,610 price tag.

familiar face behind the wheel [courtesy of TV commercials] they would sign up for one right on the spot. I drove to my local shopping center one day, and a big crowd gathered around me and my convertible. You would have thought I was giving away $10 bills! It didn't take a genius to see that this car was creating a great deal of excitement.

"Back at the office, we decided to skip the research. Our attitude was: 'Let's just build it. We won't make any money, but it'll be great publicity. If we're lucky, we'll break even.... Turned out, we sold 23,000 the first year instead of the three thousand we had planned.

"Before long, GM and Ford were bringing out convertibles of their own. In other words, little old Chrysler was

now leading the way instead of bringing up the rear."

To this, a few additions and corrections. Chrysler wasn't alone in the convertible's 1982 revival. That same year, Buick introduced a new soft-top Riviera, the first ever, converted from Riv coupes by Cars & Concepts, the Brighton, Michigan, design and fabrication house that assisted Chrysler with its convertibles.

More importantly, in this writer's opinion, Iacocca omits a big reason Chrysler returned to ragtops: It needed something different to maintain momentum. Its all-important K-car compacts, the front-drive Dodge Aries and Plymouth Reliant, had garnered considerable attention on their 1981 model-year debut (mainly because the firm's position was so pre-

carious) and exciting new minivan and sports-coupe derivatives were in the wings (back then it seemed Chrysler couldn't leak new-model plans too soon or too fast). But the bread-and-butter Ks, as one writer put it, "could barely stifle a yawn." Convertible versions would help keep the spotlight on them while suggesting that Chrysler did indeed have a future.

Then too, the decision to offer convertibles had almost certainly been made by the time that crowd gathered around Chairman Lee's one-off. It was not a case of, as some joked about the K, "if this one sells, we'll build another one." Also, he must have meant the summer of '81, as his production convertibles were in dealer showrooms by the summer of '82, having been introduced that spring. And he must have

Chrysler Corporation, seeking an inexpensive way to broaden and glamourize its product line, became the first of the Big Three to get back into the convertible business. Based on the then-new K-cars, both Chrysler and Dodge debuted soft tops in mid-1982, and immediately took sales leadership. Seen here is the '82 Dodge 400, powered by a 2.6-liter four, but a turbo option arrived for 1984 to liven things up a bit.

been driving the prototype Reliant convertible that was displayed at the Detroit and Chicago auto shows in early '81, shortly after the Ks were in production.

But never mind: The convertible was back. Propitiously introduced in time for the annual spring sales push (one of Iacocca's favored sales tactics at Ford in the Sixties), Chrysler fielded a pair based on the new-for-'82 Chrysler LeBaron/Dodge 400. The first of many K-car variations to come, these were plusher, pricier and slightly longer than Aries/Reliant but otherwise identical, riding the same 100.3-inch-wheelbase chassis. The ragtops came with the 2.6-liter Mitsubishi four optional on lesser models, and with its associated three-speed automatic transaxle.

Business proved good, if not booming. (Iacocca's claimed 23,000 sales reflects combined LeBaron/400 volume for 1982 *and* '83.) But it was strong enough that Chrysler's St. Louis plant, which supplied the coupes for convertible conversion, began converting some itself when C&C couldn't keep up. Eventually, St. Louis took over the job entirely.

The auto editors of CONSUMER GUIDE® first tried one of these reborn convertibles, a Dodge 400, in late 1982. "It's still a real kick to put the top down and go cruising on a sunny day," they wrote. "The standard power top worked flawlessly.... Expensive-looking vinyl trim and carpets gave the interior a quality appearance and are standard [but the] dashboard comes only with speedometer and fuel gauge

and long pieces of fake wood.... The test model had only 2000 miles on it [yet] the top was already wrinkled [and the] zip-out plastic back window was starting to scratch and will probably need replacement before the last payment is made."

Things weren't much better on the road: "With the top up, wind whistles through the interior at highway speed. Wind and road noises combine with body shakes for a lot of racket. There are large blind spots to the rear... doors feel heavy from reinforcing and are hard to close tightly. Chrysler claims the [conversion] adds little weight, but the car feels sluggish and underpowered.... The convertible conversion eats up so much rear seat room that it's nearly impossible for adults to sit in back."

The editors admitted that most of these faults were typical of convertibles since time immemorial, and that the true ragtop nut would probably be willing to put up with them. But their conclusions were still mixed: "Viewed as a car for show, it's a great success. The striking appearance nearly disguises its K-car origins. As a car for go, it leaves a great deal to be desired."

Chrysler set about making its ragtops more desirable. First came a new Town & Country model for '83, the first open T&C since 1949 and a car that seemed sure to please those with a sense of history. True, its flanks were adorned with plastic instead of real tree-wood, but even the original had

169

used mahogany decals from mid-1947. Maintaining tradition, the new T&C was expensive—$16,300 initially—though that was almost exactly equivalent (in much-inflated dollars) to the '49 model's $3995. Newly optional for both ragtop LeBarons was a handsome Mark Cross package comprising leather interior trim (unfortunately festooned with "MC" logos), cast-aluminum road wheels, more instruments (electronic, alas) and more, yours for $2800.

The '84 LeBaron/400 convertibles answered some of CG's objections. A more compact top mechanism liberated additional back-seat space, new roll-down rear quarter windows reduced the big over-the-shoulder blind spot, and the backlight switched from plastic to glass. Dodge 400s became 600s for '84, by which time a new 600ES Turbo convertible was available with the blown, 147-horsepower version of Chrysler's own 2.2-liter four. A special sport/handling suspension package was standard, bringing larger front and rear anti-roll bars, "high-control" shocks, firmed-up power steering, and 60-series performance tires on "Swiss cheese" aluminum wheels. Base price was near $14,200.

For 1986, LeBaron and 600 were slightly restyled at each end and offered a second engine option: the new

2.5-liter version of Chrysler's "Trans-4," smoother than the base 2.2 by dint of a Mitsubishi-style balancer shaft. But then both these "CV-Series" convertibles were canceled for '87, leaving Dodge dealers with no ragtops and Chrysler-Plymouth stores with a handsome new LeBaron. (As a sop to the Dodge boys, Chrysler canceled its Laser version of Dodge's Daytona sports coupe, which was heavily face-lifted for good measure.)

There was a reason, of course: greater distinction between Dodge and C-P through fewer shared models. And the new J-body LeBaron is Chrysler's best-looking convertible yet: smooth, rounded and aerodynamic, a bit Avanti-like astern—testimony to the talent of today's Chrysler stylists under Tom Gale. The T&C treatment didn't suit the new look and has been abandoned, but base and "Premium" convertibles are offered with the usual equipment and standard 2.5 engine.

Still, this is basically a K-car underneath, and CONSUMER GUIDE® hasn't been "overwhelmed by the LeBaron's road manners, interior materials or assembly quality"—nor the turbo 2.2, which "generates 46 more horsepower [than the 2.5] and a good deal more noise as well." But Chrysler will reportedly slot in a V-6 in a year or two.

The Dodge 400 convertible (*top*) went largely unchanged for 1983, but faced new competition from the Pontiac 2000 ragtop (*right*), a conversion done by the American Sunroof Company. Mustang's body (*above*) accommodated convertible styling nicely.

Competitors were fairly quick to chime in with convertibles of their own: Buick, as mentioned, for '82; Chevrolet and Ford for 1983; Pontiac and Cadillac (the latter to the ire of two lawyers with '76 Eldos—see previous chapter) for '84. Still, Chrysler gets the credit for reviving ragtops—ironic, as it had never been able to sell that many in the old days. Of course, this was the "New Chrysler Corporation." And indeed, the Chrysler marque has been among Detroit's top three convertible producers in every year since 1982; in '85 it was first.

Chrysler and the others were only responding to the small but steady demand for American convertibles that had been met by aftermarket conversions in the factory ragtop's six-year absence. Given the economics of automaking in the Eighties and the fact that convertibles always sell in relatively low volume, it was only natural that they'd turn to the same companies for design and manufacturing assistance in building their own new models. Thus, except for Chrysler's, today's new-generation ragtops are not "factory built" the way the last Seventies models were, though you still buy them through your local dealer.

Convertibles have yet to reappear in Lincoln-Mercury showrooms, but Ford Division has had great success with them, running with the ball tossed by Lee Iacocca. In fact, Ford has been America's leading convertible producer in four of the past five model years (1983–84 and 1986–87), averaging about 20,000 annually. Of course, they're all Mustangs.

To steal some of Chrysler's thunder, Ford first displayed its reborn ragtop as a 1982 prototype, but didn't start production until the facelifted '83 Mustangs were ready. Bowing in top-line GLX trim at around $11,000, this new flip-top Ford featured roll-down rear side windows, standard power top and glass backlight. As with other Mustangs, buyers could choose from normal and turbocharged 2.3-liter fours, 3.8 V-6 and the beloved 302-cubic-inch (4.9-liter) small-block V-8.

A rearranged '84 Mustang lineup presented three convertibles: base LX and two new GTs, V-8 and Turbo. The last, fussier to drive and costlier than the V-8 version, garnered few orders: a mere 600 or so that year (plus 2450 coupes). Exit Turbo GT. The other two

Buick re-entered the convertible business from mid-1982 to 1985, building a total of 3898 Rivieras, here (*above*) an '84. Chrysler dolled-up its LeBaron soft-top with woodgrain body sides, making this '84 a Town & Country (*right*).

would continue, and are with us yet.

All Mustangs got another nose job for '85, V-8 models another 25 horses. For '86, the 302 gained port fuel injection and a healthy 40 extra pounds-feet torque. Come 1987 and Mustang was again facelifted, in line with Ford's "aero look"; the V-6 option vanished. The '88s? Virtual reruns.

Except for the usual higher prices, which these days start at $13,700 for the LX soft-top, $16,600 for the GT. That seems steep, but the GT remains a real bargain in ragtop performance, adding the 225-bhp V-8, five-speed manual transmission, firm suspension, limited-slip differential and

special trim and equipment to the LX spec. If the latest GT styling is a bit much for you (it is for some), you can always order the more conservative LX, specify the V-8 and GT chassis upgrades, and save a few bucks. Otherwise, you'll get a lowly non-turbo four that's been around since the Pinto—and feels it.

The ragtop Riviera, introduced almost simultaneously with Highland Park's first soft-tops, was a logical step for the personal-luxury Buick. It was a good "image move" too, since Cadillac and Oldsmobile didn't immediately snip tops from their E-body cars, Eldorado and Toronado. Yet the Riviera

didn't sell, so it didn't last long, being dropped after model year '85 (when production was only 400 units) after about 4000 had been built. One reason was high price: $25,000 base, about $10,000 more than a comparable Riviera coupe.

Performance—or rather the lack of it—was another problem. Said *Collectible Automobile*® magazine: "Though Buick's 125-horsepower 4.1-liter V-6 was standard, it didn't move this 3800-pound car with much gusto, aggravated by the tall 'economy' gearing of GM's four-speed Turbo Hydramatic, the only transmission available. Fortunately, the extra-cost 140-bhp 307 V-8 (imported from Olds) was a no-charge convertible option, and we suspect most of the ragtops had it. Buick's 3.8 turbo V-6 was also theoretically available, but its accompanying T-Type equipment wasn't, so it's likely few, if any, convertibles were so endowed." As it was, the 4.1 gave you 0-60 mph in about 15 seconds and "economy" of 14 mpg.

At least the Riv was plush and quiet, thanks to a velour interior and extensive sound insulation. But *CA's* editorial colleagues at CONSUMER GUIDE® complained about ride comfort: "All-independent suspension gives fine ride control on good roads, but wavy surfaces make the body rise and fall like a merry-go-round horse."

What really killed the open Riviera

Opposite page, top: By sleight of hand, the Dodge 400 convertible became the 600 for 1984. Although it shared most components with the 600, the '84 Chrysler LeBaron (*above*) featured a more formal front end appearance. Cadillac faced lawsuits when, after building its "last" convertible in 1976, brought out the 1984 Eldorado Biarritz ragtop (*bottom row*). It disappeared after 1985.

Neither the Chrysler LeBaron (*above*) nor Dodge 600 (*below*) changed much for 1985. The hood vents indicate turbo power, and the 600's ES Turbo package included a sport/handling suspension and aluminum road wheels. Best known of the neo classic automakers, Excalibur (*right*) offers a modern drivetrain, high prices, and exclusivity.

was GM's switch to even-smaller new E-body cars for 1986. Buyers truly rebelled at their high prices and styling that aped that of much cheaper GM models. It's doubtful that convertibles would have helped sales very much, as they would surely have cost more than the coupes. The official explanation for why the new Riv/Eldo/Toro had none was that a convertible conversion would have rendered the coupe's back seat unacceptably small. Fair enough, but GM had other plans, more of which anon.

Cadillac was rather slow to follow with a convertible version of its Riviera-cousin Eldorado. The reason was certainly not because it once promised to build no more convertibles but rather because of the Riviera's slow sales, which must have made Cadillac managers hesitate.

But they finally took the plunge for 1984 with a new ragtop Eldo, offered only in uplevel Biarritz trim (apt, that).

Like the Riv, it would vanish after '85. At $32,105 base, it was the most expensive U.S. production convertible ever built to that time, though price didn't kill it as much as the advent of that new E-body and the luxury market's continuing desertion to imports.

Cadillac has recently tried to stem the import tide—and polish up a quite tarnished image—with yet another, even costlier convertible: the Allante. Aimed at the big-bucks Mercedes 560SL (over $61,000 by 1988), Cadillac's first modern-day production two-seater bowed with great fanfare for 1987 on a shortened (99.4-inch-wheelbase) Eldorado chassis with modified mechanicals. Power is supplied by the division's 4.1-liter transverse V-8 (as used in other front-drive Cadillacs through 1986) with multi-point (instead of single-point) fuel injection, roller valve lifters, high-flow cylinder heads and tuned intake manifold providing 170 bhp.

The Allante's tasteful but conservative styling comes from Italy's renowned Pininfarina, which also builds the bodywork and ships it to Detroit (by air!) from a new factory near Turin. Aluminum hood and trunklid are fixed to a galvanized unit steel structure. Standard equipment is predictably complete, and includes an SL-style lift-off hardtop to supplement the folding roof. The only option is a cellular telephone installed in a lockable between-seats bin and featuring the industry's first retractable AM/FM/telephone antenna.

Though a capable tourer and an entirely new breed of Cadillac, the Allante has so far failed to make the hoped-for impression. Cadillac predicted 1987 model-year sales of 4000 units but got only 1651; for the first full production year, deliveries totaled just 2500 out of a planned 7000. The result: an embarrassing pile-up of unsold cars, rebates to clear it—and a

Clockwise from top left: 1986 Chevrolet Cavalier RS, '86 Chrysler LeBaron with Town & Country trim, '86 Dodge 600, '86 Pontiac Sunbird SE, '87 Corvette. The Cavalier RS could be had with GM's 2.8-liter V-6, greatly enhancing performance. Those who wanted more poke from their Pontiac could order the GT package, adding a turbo 1.8 engine, rally suspension and gauges, and more.

further blow to Cadillac's prestige. *Automotive News* went so far as to call Allante the 1987 "Flop of the Year," though division chief John O. Grettenberger dismissed this and wide coverage of the car's slow start as "just the latest round of GM bashing."

Still, there are undeniable problems. As *AutoWeek*'s Chris Sawyer pointed out, the Allante is expensive for what it is—$54,000 at announcement, rising to $56,500 with the unchanged '88—yet it depreciates by a third the minute it leaves the showroom. The SL, by contrast, *appreciates* in value. Then too, Allante has been plagued by the sort of niggling troubles not common in Mercedes: wind and water leaks around the top, miscellaneous squeaks and rattles, engine oil leaks, horns that don't work and heaters that work too well.

Worst of all, Allante buyers are, "in almost every respect except [higher] income level, the same clientele to whom Cadillac has customarily appealed." The Allante may yet succeed both as a car and an image-booster. But as Sawyer notes, "The fact remains that no matter how rough the sledding, GM has left itself only one option if it is to have any hope of resurrecting the Cadillac name. It must stand and fight."

Oldsmobile, which prospered with convertibles so often, has built none since its 1975 Delta 88 Royale. Pontiac and Chevy have—J-car Cavalier and Sunbird models, respectively—but the results to date are inconclusive.

After testing public reaction with a prototype, Chevy began selling the Cavalier convertible in limited numbers beginning late in the '83 model year, when only 627 were built. But the ragtop was more readily available and in a greater variety of color and trim combinations for '84. It sold as a sporty Type-10 (which formerly meant only a hatchback coupe) at just over $11,000 base. All '84 Cavaliers were handsomely facelifted with quad headlamps, cross-hatch grille and body-color bumpers.

The subcompact Cavalier has long delivered excellent mileage and—since 1984—decent performance. But it's never been cheap for its class, and price must have caused a lot of buyers to think twice about signing for a convertible. Nevertheless, Chevrolet has increased output every year since the soft-top Cav's announcement, which

In a direct attack on the Mercedes 560SL, Cadillac debuted the $54,700 Allante (*above*) for 1987, featuring Pininfarina-designed-and-built bodies airlifted from Italy for final assembly in Detroit. Pontiac continued its Sunbird convertible for '87, seen here as the sporty GT (*right*). *Opposite page*: Although still called LeBaron, Chrysler's convertible received a sleek new body in mid-1987 (*top*). The perky little Renault Alliance DL (*bottom*) was the lowest price convertible sold in America in 1986.

is more than most convertible makers can claim. The '87 total was 16,451, more than half of the 27,000-plus divisional total that made Chevy "USA-1" in convertibles for the first time since 1974.

Type-10 Cavaliers were renamed RS for 1986. Standard power remained the dull 2.0-liter overhead-valve four used since Cavalier's birth, but the convertible was optionally offered with the fine 2.8-liter Chevy V-6 from the new neo-muscle Z-24 hatchback. An extra-cost Getrag-designed five-speed manual transaxle was announced that year, but didn't become available until '87 when "Generation II" improvements were applied to both engines.

A more substantial facelift considerably changed Cavalier's looks for '88. Even better, the RS convertible was made a Z-24, with standard V-6, "handling" suspension, all-season performance tires on aluminum wheels, and the sportiest premium interior. The one sour note was price, now $16,000 minimum. That seemed a lot for a small car, even a rapid, roadable ragtop.

Symbolic of the convertible's resurgence was the mid-1986 debut of the first Corvette roadster in 11 years. Announced just in time to pace the Indy 500, it was based on the slightly smaller (96.2-inch-wheelbase) and lighter sixth-generation Corvette, introduced as a targa-top coupe in early 1983 for model year '84. It naturally shared most of the coupe's pluses: sleek styling, sophisticated all-independent suspension, powerful 350 V-8, Bosch antilock braking system (from 1986) and more practical packaging. It also inherited most of the minuses: rocky ride, gimmicky electronic instruments, indifferent workmanship, and record prices—a little over $33,000 on introduction. Yet despite that, the reborn roadster (a misnomer; it remained a true convertible) sold quite well. Chevy moved 7264 for the balance of the '86 season and 10,625 for '87.

The sixth-generation Vette had been designed with a convertible in mind, and some of the necessary stiffening measures engineered for the roofless version showed up in the '87 coupe to answer complaints about body shake in earlier models. Specifically, K-braces were added to connect the front frame crossmember with the chassis siderails, door latches were strengthened, a crossmember applied behind the cockpit, and an X-brace tacked-on amidships. The convertible had slightly different rear-quarter contours and its own suspension tuning, which was midway between the coupe's stock setup and Z-51 handling option.

Recalling the original '53 Vette, the new roadster arrived with a manual top that folded beneath a rigid cover. The '86s were all considered Indy Pace Car Replicas and thus came with facsimile owner-applied decals (Detroit never seems to tire of this). Unlike previous commemorative Corvettes, however, the full range of factory body colors was available (the actual pacers were painted bright yellow).

Though the revived ragtop Vette was criticized for encroaching on exoticar price territory, its fans could argue that there was nothing else quite like it at any price. They were—and are—correct. Punting one along a smooth, twisty two-lane on a sunny day with the top down is the very essence of what American cars are all about.

And, like the coupe, it just keeps getting better. Adoption of Tuned Port Injection (replacing the 1982-vintage

dual throttle-body system) had lifted the venerable Chevy small-block from 205 to 230 SAE net horsepower by the time the roadster arrived. For 1987, roller valve lifters and other internal changes added 10 more, while raising torque to an impressive 345 pounds-feet (versus 290 the previous year). Result: 0-60-mph times of close to six seconds flat.

Model year '88 brings more tweaks that add another five horses for 245 total. Equally welcome are new-design wheels concealing larger and thicker all-disc brakes—which grow larger still with the newly optional 17-inch wheels that wear huge P275/40ZR-17 tires rated for speeds in excess of 149 mph. Talk about "wind in your hair" driving! Of course, few owners will ever approach that speed—or should—but we can all be grateful for the return of a great American tradition. *Vive la Vette!*

Chevy took more than four years to answer the open-air Mustang directly, but its new Camaro convertible, arriving in January 1987, cheered dealers and enthusiasts alike. Another factory-approved conversion (by Automobile

Specialty Company, a division of Detroit-based American Sunroof), it was offered in the same four guises as that year's closed Camaro: high-performance IROC-Z and Z-28, LT (Luxury Touring) and base V-6 Sport Coupe (was the last thus a "Sport Coupe convertible?"). Only 4000 were scheduled to be built that model year, all suitably reinforced to accommodate the soft top and engines that ran to the IROC's 5.7-liter, 220-bhp injected 350 V-8. Base price was near $14,400, though a full-tilt IROC set you back another $3000 or more.

As it had with the T&C, 600ES Turbo and Riviera ragtops, *Collectible Automobile®* was quick to single out the convertible Camaro as a future collectible, the IROC in particular: "Even taking the rough ride and lousy gas mileage into consideration, the IROC-Z convertible is a blue-chip investment. Buy one now and enjoy it, take meticulous care of it, and it will return more than its original price somewhere down the road, and likely sooner than most people think.... If history is a guide, demand will soon exceed supply...."

Possibly, though in today's unpredictable market, as Sam Goldwyn said, "all predictions are dangerous—especially about the future." It'll be interesting to see whether Chevy can sell as many '88 convertible Camaros as ASC can supply. The cars are certainly no problem. Though the LT and Z-28 are gone now, the '88 IROC and base models are the cleanest- and best-looking of the third-generation Camaros; they also boast upgraded trim and more attractive equipment. But like the inevitability of death and taxes, prices are higher: at this writing a minimum $16,250 for the base model, $18,000 for the IROC—the real reason to "buy one now," as *CA* advised.

Pontiac began offering soft-top Sunbirds soon after the convertible Cavalier went on sale, but it wouldn't have Chevy's success. In 1986, for example, the Cav outsold the Bird 13 to three despite similar price tags (though possibly because of the greater number and higher volume of Chevy dealerships).

First cataloged in the up level LE series for 1984, the convertible was of-

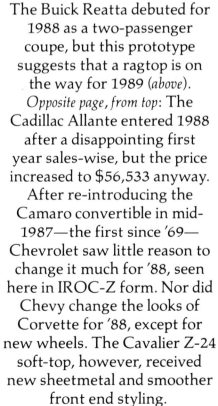

The Buick Reatta debuted for 1988 as a two-passenger coupe, but this prototype suggests that a ragtop is on the way for 1989 (*above*). *Opposite page*, *from top*: The Cadillac Allante entered 1988 after a disappointing first year sales-wise, but the price increased to $56,533 anyway. After re-introducing the Camaro convertible in mid-1987—the first since '69—Chevrolet saw little reason to change it much for '88, seen here in IROC-Z form. Nor did Chevy change the looks of Corvette for '88, except for new wheels. The Cavalier Z-24 soft-top, however, received new sheetmetal and smoother front end styling.

Buick built a convertible prototype of the front-drive '88 Regal (*top*)—it may go into production. The Oldsmobile Cutlass Supreme, 1988 Indy 500 Pace Car (*above*), might see a ragtop version, too. Note the '49 Olds Pace Car (*center*).

fered with the same three engines as other Sunbirds: Cavalier ohv four and normal and turbocharged versions of the new Opel-designed 1.8-liter overhead-cam four supplied to Pontiac (and

Buick and Olds for their J-cars) by GM do Brasil. The LE became an SE for '86, when Pontiac added a new GT convertible with semi-hidden headlamps, rear spoiler, the turbo 1.8 and beefier

Rally suspension. Both ohc engines grew to 2.0 liters as the main change for '87, while '88 brought a Cavalier-style "taillift" and an end to the soft-top SE.

With all this, Sunbird convertible sales have improved somewhat since '84, and Pontiac insists its convertible will continue. But at just 3452 for 1987, it may not be around much longer.

Finally, a rather curious re-entry to the convertible ranks in the Eighties: good old never-say-die American Motors, by then in the hands of France's Renault—but only temporarily. As many expected, when the going got tough, Renault got going—out the door. AMC now belongs to Chrysler but lives on in spirit as the new Jeep-Eagle Division, selling the same specialty 4×4s and Renault-designed sedans *sans* diamond logos.

But before its 1987 takeover, AMC gave us a convertible version of the unmemorable front-drive Renault Alliance subcompact. Introduced for 1985, two years behind Alliance sedans and Encore hatchbacks, it actually put American Motors in fourth place for the first time since the Sixties—in convertible sales, that is. A factory-built job and AMC's first topless car since 1968, it was the cheapest convertible in the country: just over $10,000 without options. It was also remarkably light for a convertible: 2184 pounds, about 200 up on the two-door sedan. For $1000 more than the base L model, customers could have a DL, with better trim, reclining seats, five-speed overdrive manual transmission, extra insulation and other amenities. It was no road-burner with the standard 1.4-liter four, but was more acceptable with that year's newly enlarged 1.7-liter option.

As anybody could have told AMC—and might have, come to that—the Alliance would have had to have been 20 times the car it was to be a long-term success. While it wasn't all *that* bad, it competed in a market segment full of quicker, quieter, better-built cars. After two fairly strong years, sales plunged in 1985 owing to Japanese competition, a market swing to more expensive models, stable fuel prices, and Renault's poor U.S. reputation (something Alliance did little to improve). Convertibles suffered right along with other models, dropping from 7143 to 1651 units for '86.

Still pushing water uphill, AMC came back for '87 with "pocket rocket" GTA models: a $9000 two-door sedan and a $13,000 convertible. A new 95-bhp 2.0-liter four delivered 0-60 in under 10 seconds, and an uprated suspension provided near sports-car cornering power (though claimed lateral acceleration was optimistic at 0.89G). But again, Alliance just didn't have enough of the "right stuff"—or perhaps it had too much of the wrong stuff. In any case, it was the first thing to go when Chrysler hung its sign on AMC's Kenosha, Wisconsin, factory (which it soon closed). Which only means that the GTA convertible stands to become a collectors item someday, though a minor one to be sure.

Of more lasting importance, perhaps, are some great American convertibles to come: one from Lincoln-Mercury; one, possibly two, from Buick. Definitely due for 1989 is a new open version of Buick's Riviera-based Reatta two-seat luxury coupe, introduced in early '88. A prototype of this pretty car has already been widely seen in photos, official and otherwise. If the convertible is anything like the coupe,

it should be well worth waiting for: smooth, reasonably peppy, very practical for a two-seater, and loaded with all the goodies.

Buick is less certain about a soft-top version of its new-for-'88 front-drive Regal, one of the vaunted GM-10 intermediate coupes. However, a one-off received good reviews at various auto shows and press functions in early 1988, so we'd guess that chances are better than 50/50 for a production model. Chevy V-6 power, all-independent suspension, standard four-wheel disc brakes and distinctively Buick styling (GM's learned its lesson: no more clones) make this another one to anticipate with relish.

An equally exciting prospect is the new Mercury Capri set for '89. No longer a "bubbleback" Mustang, it's a small and sporty open 2+2 derived from Mazda's latest front-drive 323 subcompact and built by Ford Australia. The 323's 1.6-liter single-overhead-cam four will be offered in 82-bhp normally aspirated form, and with turbocharger for an XR2 performance model packing 100-plus bhp. Both will mount transversely in a slick Ford-designed body with manual top and, despite the "road-

ster" description in spy reports, roll-up windows. If L-M can bring it in at the rumored $11,000 base price, this new Capri ought to sell like gangbusters. But then, it *is* a convertible.

And since 1927, that's been one of the nicest things a car can be. Innate appeal has enabled the convertible to survive, despite market upheavals, repeated obituaries and critiques by self-appointed experts.

One of the last, writing in the Philadelphia *Inquirer* on the imagined death of the convertible back in '76, inadvertently pinpointed why the thing just won't go away. Convertibles, he said, evoke memories of "movies with Andy Hardy and his college chums packed into a bulging convertible...of parking high in the hills with the stars blinking above and the city lights below. And we were Jimmy Stewart and June Allyson, or we were Clark Gable and Carole Lombard. Romance was alive in the land."

Today we may be Robert Redford and Brooke Shields, themselves ragtop devotees. Assaults of the ignorant notwithstanding, romance is still alive in this land. And as long as convertibles are around, it always will be.

PRODUCTION FIGURES

It is fascinating to trace the ups and downs of convertible production, but determining exact counts is quite difficult. Industry figures have been commonly nebulous, or estimated, or sometimes (as for 1927–30 and 1936–40) nonexistent. Moreover, even some sources that do exist may disagree, forcing the researcher either to accept one source or strike an average.

The author arrived at most estimates herein by dividing the total figure for each make (including estimates where figures are not available) by model year production. While this yields a decent approximation, it cannot be exact because some manufacturers quoted calendar year rather than model year output. (The high percentage in 1942 is an anomaly, but this war-abbreviated year should never be used as a yardstick anyway.)

Where we are blessed with several sources, the best industry records have been accepted: Polk's over *Ward's* or *Automotive News*, for example. (The latter's 1987 *Data Book* actually transposes the columns for convertibles vs. two-tone paint jobs!) Between 1947 and 1976 I paid serious attention to the statistics published by R. Perry Zavitz in the Spring 1976 (No. 15) issue of *The Milestone Car*, on the grounds that his research was more recent as well as more painstaking than the rest.

I would appreciate reader comment and corrections. Address: Publications International, Ltd., 7373 North Cicero Ave., Lincolnwood, IL 60646.

—Richard M. Langworth

Calendar Year Production

Cal. Year	Total Number Convertibles	Percent of Total Prod.
1927	2,600*	0.01
1928	10,000*	0.02
1929	25,000*	0.06
1930	40,000*	1.5
1931	85,314	4.2
1932	42,103	3.6
1933	22,823	1.4
1934	38,905	1.7
1935	41,917	1.2
1936	40,000*	1.1
1937	35,000*	0.9
1938	27,000*	1.4
1939	37,000*	1.3
1940	55,000*	1.5
1941	98,335	2.7

Calendar Year Production

Year	Production	%
1942	20,000*	9.4
1946	45,000*	2.1
1947	173,863	4.9
1948	196,597	5.0
1949	215,635	4.2
1950	208,090	3.1
1951	143,388	2.7
1952	100,116	2.3
1953	154,500*	2.5
1954	131,500*	2.7
1955	212,000*	3.0
1956	210,000*	3.4
1957	266,000*	4.3
1958	193,717	4.6
1959	257,200*	4.6
1960	313,700*	4.7
1961	271,600*	4.9
1962	437,659	6.3
1963	489,824	6.4
1964	498,494	6.3
1965	509,415	5.5
1966	394,679	4.6
1967	306,078	4.1
1968	276,731	3.1
1969	201,997	2.5
1970	91,863	1.4
1971	87,725	1.0
1972	61,655	0.7
1973	50,837	0.5
1974	27,955	0.5
1975	8,950	0.001
1976	14,000	0.002
1977	0	0.0
1978	0	0.0
1979	0	0.0
1980	0	0.0
1981	0	0.0
1982	9,834	0.2
1983	40,594	0.7
1984	57,501	0.7
1985	63,255	0.8
1986	76,519	1.0
1987	50,375	0.7

*estimate

Leading Producers by Model Year

1927	1928	1929
Buick	Buick	Ford
Chrysler	Chrysler	Dodge
Cadillac	Packard	Buick

1930	1931	1932
Ford	Chevrolet	Chevrolet
Olds	Ford	Plymouth
Dodge	Olds	Ford

1933	1934	1935
Ford	Ford	Ford
Plymouth	Plymouth	Olds
Chevrolet	Chevrolet	Plymouth

1936	1937	1938
Ford	Ford	Ford
Buick	Buick	Buick
Chevrolet	Plymouth	Chevrolet

1939	1940	1941
Ford	Chevrolet	Buick
Plymouth	Ford	Chevrolet
Buick	Buick	Ford
Chevrolet	Plymouth	Plymouth

1942	1946	1947
Buick	Ford	Buick
Ford	Buick	Chevrolet
Plymouth	Mercury	Ford
Dodge	Chevrolet	Olds

1948	1949	1950
Buick	Ford	Ford
Chevrolet	Chevrolet	Chevrolet
Olds	Buick	Pontiac
Pontiac	Olds	Buick
Studebaker	Mercury	Olds

1951	1952	1953
Ford	Ford	Ford
Chevrolet	Chevrolet	Chevrolet
Buick	Buick	Olds
Plymouth	Olds	Buick
Pontiac	Pontiac	Pontiac

1954	1955	1956
Ford	Ford	Ford
Chevrolet	Chevrolet	Chevrolet
Buick	Buick	Buick
Olds	Pontiac	Olds
Pontiac	Olds	Pontiac

1957	1958	1959
Ford	Chevrolet	Chevrolet
Chevrolet	Ford	Ford
Olds	Olds	Pontiac
Buick	Pontiac	Buick
Pontiac	Buick	Olds

1960	1961	1962
Chevrolet	Chevrolet	Chevrolet
Ford	Ford	Ford
Pontiac	Pontiac	Pontiac
Buick	Buick	Buick
Olds	Cadillac	Olds

1963	1964	1965
Chevrolet	Chevrolet	Ford
Ford	Ford	Chevrolet
Pontiac	Pontiac	Pontiac
Buick	Buick	Buick
Olds	Olds	Olds

1966	1967	1968
Ford	Chevrolet	Chevrolet
Chevrolet	Ford	Pontiac
Pontiac	Pontiac	Ford
Buick	Buick	Buick
Olds	Olds	Olds

1969	1970	1971
Chevrolet	Chevrolet	Chevrolet
Pontiac	Olds	Olds
Ford	Ford	Ford
Olds	Buick	Buick
Buick	Pontiac	Pontiac

1972	1973	1974
Chevrolet	Chevrolet	Chevrolet
Olds	Ford	Cadillac
Ford	Cadillac	Olds
Buick	Olds	Buick
Pontiac	Buick	Pontiac

1975	1982	1983
Olds	Dodge	Ford
Chevrolet	Chrysler	Chrysler
Cadillac	Buick	Dodge
Buick	—	Buick
Pontiac	—	Chevrolet

1984	1985	1986
Ford	Chrysler	Ford
Chrysler	Dodge	Chrysler
Dodge	Ford	Dodge
Chevrolet	AMC	Chevrolet
Pontiac	Chevrolet	Pontiac

1987		
Chevrolet		
Ford		
Chrysler		
Pontiac		
AMC		

Convertible Production

It is not possible to obtain model year production figures for each make building convertibles. At various times, some makes record calendar year figures, sales or registration totals, but not model year production—the figure which most enthusiasts care most about.

Estimates based on known convertible percentages of overall model year output are therefore indicated with an asterisk (*), while calendar year figures are indicated with two asterisks (**).

In order to show when convertibles were being produced by each maker, I have also resorted to two other designations: "NA" (figures of any kind not available) and "0" (the make was in production, but did not produce convertibles.
—RML

Model Year	1927	1928	1929	1930	1931	1932	1933	1934	1935	1936	1937
Auburn-C-D		NA	NA	NA	NA	NA	NA	NA	NA	NA	
Buick	2,373	6,555	2,112	0	1,540	1,696	899	1,660	1,660	3,646	6,767
Cadillac	NA	NA	NA	NA	NA	NA	NA	NA	NA	NA	NA
Chevrolet					28,711	NA	4,276	3,276	0	3,629	1,724
Chrysler	200*	1,778	1,500*	1,900*	2,700*	1,600*	2,296	1,150	101	1,252	2,085
De Soto				700*	1,000*	1,000*	544	0	226	465	1,418
Dodge			2,400*	2,000*	750*	500*	1,658	1,239	950	2,275	1,818
Essex						NA	NA				
Ford			16,421**	25,868**	16,665**	8,205	8,800*	15,500*	21,536	19,669	14,562
Franklin		NA	NA	NA	NA	NA	NA	NA			
Graham		NA	NA	NA	0	NA	NA	NA	NA	NA	NA
Hudson						NA	NA	NA	NA	NA	NA
Hupp			NA	NA	NA	NA	NA	NA	0	0	0
La Salle		NA	NA	NA	NA	NA	NA	NA	NA	NA	NA
Lincoln	20*	NA	NA	200*	300*	50*	200*	275*	100*	100*	50*
Nash		NA	NA								
Olds				3,006	3,501	1,117	584	915	2,508	3,067	2,347
Packard		NA	NA	NA	NA	NA	NA	NA	NA	NA	NA
Plymouth				550*	725*	8,326	6,630	4,482	2,308	3,297	3,110
Pontiac			NA	NA	NA	NA	NA	NA	NA	NA	NA
Studebaker		NA	NA	NA	NA	NA	NA	NA	0	0	0
Terraplane								NA	NA	NA	NA

Model Year	1938	1939	1940	1941	1942	1946	1947	1948	1949
Buick	4,895	5,659	9,729	19,403	4,788	8,574	40,371	30,520	30,354
Cadillac	396	564	354	3,500	308	1,342	6,755	5,450	8,000
Chevrolet	2,787	0	11,820	15,296	1,182	4,508	28,443	20,471	32,392
Chrysler	959	0	1,900*	5,727	975	500*	5,766**	6,215**	4,700**
De Soto	519	0	1,085	2,937	568	300*	2,969**	3,257*	3,500**
Dodge	833	0	2,100	3,554	1,185	500*	3,823**	3,826**	2,500**
Ford	7,445	13,983	10,000*	12,800*	3,000*	17,568	24,409	12,061	51,133
Frazer									44*
Graham	0	0	0	0					
Hudson	NA	NA	NA	1,052**	NA	1,175*	1,823**	1,188**	3,119**
Hupp	0	0	0	0					

*estimate   **calendar year

Convertible Production

Model Year	1938	1939	1940	1941	1942	1946	1947	1948	1949
Kaiser								66*	
La Salle	1,120	1,241	1,224						
Lincoln	1,182	946	775*	1,125	327	1,000*	1,616**	2,516**	743**
Mercury		NA	NA	4,900	1,230	6,044	10,221	7,586	16,765
Nash	NA	NA	NA	NA	0	0	0	999	0
Olds	1,659	2,186	2,757	5,297	1,000*	2,283	10,468	16,806	23,374
Packard	NA	NA	NA	NA	NA	0	0	8,868	2,127
Plymouth	1,900	6,363	6,986	10,545	2,806	NA	5,089**	6,048**	16,300**
Pontiac	NA	NA	NA	5,981**	NA	NA	10,020**	15,937**	14,795**
Studebaker	NA	NA	0	0	0	0	3,754	17,978	8,737

Model Year	1950	1951	1952	1953	1954	1955	1956	1957	1958	1959
Buick	15,223	13,126	9,906	15,991	16,409	23,863	21,676	19,018	10,110	21,429
Cadillac	6,986	6,117	6,400	8,899	8,460	12,100	10,450	10,800	8,640	12,450
Chevrolet	32,810	20,172	11,975	29,664	19,383	41,292	44,735	53,901	65,157	82,435
Chrysler	3,100	4,700*	2,400*	2,200	1,225	2,341	1,932	1,533	859	1,387
De Soto	2,900	2,600*	2,200*	1,700	1,025	1,400	2,100*	2,748	1,775	1,200*
Dodge	4,703	4,250*	2,300*	4,100	2,050	3,302	3,339	NA	NA	NA
Edsel									2,806	1,343
Ford	50,299	40,934	22,534	40,861	36,685	66,121	73,778	119,882	51,876	69,044
Franklin										
Frazer	R/S	128*								
Hudson	3,322	1,651	636	NA	NA	0	0	0		
Imperial						1	0	1,167	675	555
Kaiser	R/S	0	0	0	0	0				
Lincoln	536	857	1,191	2,372	1,951	1,487	2,447	3,676	3,048	2,195
Mercury	8,341	6,759	5,261	8,463	7,293	10,668	10,073	10,546	3,989	5,680
Nash	9,330	NA	NA	NA	NA	0	0	0		
Olds	14,025	8,322	8,706	16,289	13,252	18,156	18,142	21,829	13,860	20,900
Packard	677	2,001	963	2,268	1,263	500	276	0	0	
Plymouth	12,697	9,500*	6,150*	6,301	6,900	8,473	6,735	9,866	9,941	11,053
Pontiac	19,696	9,470	8,502	13,500	12,374**	19,762	13,510	12,789	10,455	25,941
Rambler								0	0	0
Studebaker	13,229	8,512	3,290	0	0	0	0	0	0	0

R/S = Reserialed from previous year.

Model Year	1960	1961	1962	1963	1964	1965	1966	1967	1968	1969
Buick	25,570	23,062	37,615	40,637	38,249	38,023	29,826	25,213	27,447	22,616
Cadillac	15,285	16,950	18,250	19,425	19,770	21,325	21,450	18,202	18,025	16,445
Chevrolet	90,164	73,563	127,986	155,094	150,025	134,367	100,000*	84,395	75,266	58,044
Chrysler	2,271	3,048	4,022	5,489	4,202	5,050	5,585	4,485	5,008	4,102
De Soto	0	0								

*estimate   **calendar year

Model Year	1960	1961	1962	1963	1964	1965	1966	1967	1968	1969
Dodge	8,817	4,361	6,024	16,748	NA	NA	NA	NA	NA	NA
Edsel	76									
Ford	56,622	55,130	64,286	71,875	82,156	157,085	122,247	78,525	52,345	33,874
Imperial	618	429	554	531	922	633	514	577	474	0
Lincoln	2,044	2,857	3,212	3,138	3,328	3,356	3,180	2,276	0	0
Mercury	7,587	7,053	6,804	18,273	16,524	13,803	13,879	6,357	5,875	13,436
Olds	25,385	15,477	36,607	33,368	33,181	31,478	27,000*	25,000*	25,973	27,611
Plymouth	7,080	6,948	5,865	25,333	22,523	20,924	15,512	15,486	14,132	11,933
Pontiac	34,234	30,643	59,094	62,677	72,899	72,951	62,571	63,736	53,975	38,014
Rambler	0	NA	13,497	NA	8,904	12,334	NA	1,200	0	0
Studebaker	8,571	1,981	2,681	1,015	703	0	0			

Model Year	1970	1971	1972	1973	1974	1975	1976	1977	1978	1979
AMC	0	0	0	0	0	0	0	0	0	0
Buick	16,146	8,912	8,893	5,739	3,627	5,300	0	0	0	0
Cadillac	15,172	6,800	7,975	9,315	7,600	8,950	14,000	0	0	0
Chevrolet	25,000*	16,786	17,817	13,432	10,144	12,978	0	0	0	0
Chrysler	2,201	0	0	0	0	0	0	0	0	0
Dodge	6,305	2,165	0	0	0	0	0	0	0	0
Ford	17,960	13,484	10,635	11,853	0	0	0	0	0	0
Imperial	0	0	0	0	0	0				
Lincoln	0	0	0	0	0	0	0	0	0	0
Mercury	6,113	3,440	3,169	4,449	0	0	0	0	0	0
Olds	20,543	14,442	15,471	7,088	3,716	21,038	0	0	0	0
Plymouth	6,262	1,388	0	0	0	0	0	0	0	0
Pontiac	15,676	8,368	8,050	4,447	3,000	4,519	0	0	0	0

Model Year	1980	1981	1982	1983	1984	1985	1986	1987
AMC	0	0	0	0	0	7,143	1,651	1,000*
Buick	0	0	1,248	1,750	500	400	0	0
Cadillac	0	0	0	0	3,300	2,300	0	6,000*
Chevrolet	0	0	0	627	5,486	4,108	20,313	27,076
Chrysler	0	0	3,045	9,891	16,208	20,191	19,684	8,025
Dodge	0	0	5,541	4,888	10,960	17,173	16,437	0
Ford	0	0	0	23,438	17,600	15,110	22,946	21,447
Imperial		0	0	0				
Lincoln	0	0	0	0	0	0	0	0
Mercury	0	0	0	0	0	0	0	0
Olds	0	0	0	0	0	0	0	0
Plymouth	0	0	0	0	0	0	0	0
Pontiac	0	0	0	0	3,447	3,830	2,752	3,452

*estimate   **calendar year

Index

1950 Buick Super

1949 Hudson Commodore Six